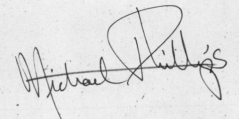

A God to Call Father

A God to Call FATHER

Discovering Intimacy with God

MICHAEL PHILLIPS

Tyndale House Publishers, Inc.
WHEATON, ILLINOIS

Published in association with the literary agency of Alive Communications, P.O. Box 49068, Colorado Springs, CO 80949.

Library of Congress Cataloging-in-Publication Data

Phillips, Michael, date
  A God to call father : discovering mountaintop intimacy with God /
Michael Phillips.
    p.   cm.
    ISBN 0-8423-1392-3
    1. God—Fatherhood.   2. God—Love.   3. Fatherhood (Theology)
4. Jesus Christ—Person and offices.   I. Title.
BT153.F3P45   1994
231'.1—dc20   94-3611

Printed in the United States of America

99   98   97   96   95   94
6   5   4   3   2

CONTENTS

PART IV

A GOD TO CALL FATHER
Glimpses of the Mountain Estate

PART V

HOME AMONG THE PEAKS
Scaling the Heights

PART VI

THE INNER CHAMBER WHERE THE FATHER'S HEART DWELLS
Finding at Last Our Eternal Dwelling Place

This is and has been
the Father's work
from the beginning—
to bring us into
the home of his heart.
This is our destiny.

———

George MacDonald

INTRODUCTION

The quest after knowledge goes in cycles.

The writing and publishing of books quite naturally, as a result, follows these ups and downs, these shifts and swings of the public appetite. Our present cycle is no exception.

Theology these days has fallen on hard times. Not just what we would call religious theology, but all realms of philosophical thought.

Like theology, the art of sound, solid, rational *thinking*—of contemplating and analyzing one's way toward growth and betterment and personal maturity—is stuck in the downside of the learning cycle. Thinking, logic, and analysis are not mental tools we learn to wield with a great deal of expertise nowadays, since these disciplines are neither taught and practiced, nor highly regarded.

Everywhere the emphasis is on the practical.

Everything is busy, fast-paced, active, and goal-and-result oriented. Don't bother with all the theories and reasons and philosophizing—let's just get on with *doing* whatever needs to be done. Get the job done. *Just do it!*

Practicality is good, as far as it goes. Certainly the Bible is practical, and Jesus was one of the most practical men who ever lived. Some of the most powerful portions of Scripture are powerful because they are so down-to-earth and practical.

Unfortunately, in our modern culture, we're so intent on racing ahead to the "doing" that we scarcely take time to build adequate intellectual foundations out of which our activities ought to grow. Logic and reason, without the capacity to live out one's conclusions, achieve nothing.

What are we doing . . . and *why?*

The rallying cry of modernism—*Just Do It!*—fails to offer much help at one very significant point—what is the *it?*

The ads never say *what* is to be done, the implication being that it really doesn't matter what you do . . . as long as you *do* it, and do it with gusto.

Modernism glorifies doing for doing's sake, without worrying about whether it *means* anything or not.

Unfortunately, Christendom has followed these

same cycles, and thus Christians have become infected with this same preoccupation with doing, often without the logical and reasoned-out theological foundation necessary to give permanent meaning and substance to all the activities of which our Christian life is comprised.

For Christians, however—especially for serious followers of Christ who desire to impact the world with the reality of gospel truth—*practical doing* has to be rooted in a theology that is correct, that makes sense, and that is well thought out.

We've lost something valuable, we Christians who live in the final years of the·twentieth century. We've lost the ability to seriously reason through the tenets of our faith. And we're in danger of losing the capacity to *think* about who God is and what his purposes are.

Did Paul, immediately after his conversion on the Damascus road, hustle out and just start *doing* it?

No. At that point he didn't even know what it was. So he isolated himself for fourteen years . . . to think, to study, and to pray about who God was and what he was about in the world.

Did C. S. Lewis, immediately after becoming a Christian, launch a new career to write and speak on behalf of the Christian faith?

No. He continued doing what he had done all his

life. He applied his God-given capacity to *think clearly* to his new faith, and he thought through every aspect of it from top to bottom. Because he did, what came later had a rock-solid foundation and, thus, a permanent, unshakable impact.

Did Francis Schaeffer move to Switzerland and immediately set up L'Abri as a haven and ministry to the intellectual student community?

No. He walked the hills and mountains alone, thinking and reasoning through his belief system. He had to know, beyond any doubt, that every part of it, down to the tiniest piece, could stand up logically and intellectually. He forced himself to examine what he believed from every conceivable angle. Thus, when the time came for him to *do* what God had called him to do, the words that came from his mouth and pen were the mature fruit of deep and well-grounded roots.

Thinking is a vital ingredient in the Christian life, out of which the balanced practicality of New Testament living is able to emerge. Without a biblically rooted theology, our Christian "doings" eventually float in a *Just Do It!* spiritual vacuum.

All this is by way of clarifying up front what kind of book this is. If you are looking for a list of x number of things you can go out and *do* tomorrow to achieve "intimacy" with God, you have picked up the wrong book.

There is not necessarily anything wrong with many of the how-to manuals flooding today's bookshelves—the twelve-steps-to-this and ten-steps-to-that and seven-steps-to-financial-security and so on. Many of those books are fine. I have even written a few of them myself. That's just not our objective here.

Practicality is a worthwhile and necessary priority. However, it is only half of the life equation for a Christian.

Here we will be dealing with the other half. We will be attempting to build a foundation. We will be orienting our *thoughts* in some new and spiritually helpful directions concerning God as Father, without preoccupying ourselves with going out and "doing."

It is impossible to know God, to obey him, to function within his family, or to understand his Word if we are thinking incorrectly about who he is.

Unfortunately, much of our thinking about him is rooted in teachings, traditions, and principles we have been taught or in impressions we have gleaned from others, rather than in our having thought and prayed through certain significant scriptural concepts for ourselves. Our knowing of God as Father, therefore, is sketchy, hazy, and incomplete.

What we will be learning together here, then, is how to think anew, in fresh, invigorating, and liberating ways, about he whom Jesus called *our Father*.

The style of our mutual quest will be more devotional than didactic. Your past experience and the frenetic times in which we live may urge you to swiftness as you read. You may strain at the pace, as a horse strains against being held back by his master's reins. We are all accustomed to horizontal movement, where speed is the necessary indication of success—the hurry of man and his anxious world. All our conditioning these days is toward urgency and haste.

But I will be moving slowly by design, laying foundations gradually and with care, not anxious to rush over important ground, pausing now and then, even for several chapters, to go over certain points several times from different perspectives. This leisurely, thoughtful pace may be difficult to get used to at first.

Our journey will be a distinctive one. It is upward, not horizontal. We will be learning to see in new ways. We will be learning to breathe a different air. And this is a process that cannot be rushed. If you can make the transition into a quieter, slower, devotional, and less-urgent frame of mind—chewing the cud of these principles, as it were, over and over as we go rather than

eagerly anxious to get quickly on to the "next pont"—
the process will be richly rewarded in the end.

You will look back when we are done and realize
what great heights you have indeed climbed, notwithstanding the more leisurely, repetitive, gradual steps of
the literary journey. You will look back on much that
we ordinarily consider "practical teaching" as the mere
going around in urgently-paced circles of what we
already know rather than moving higher and deeper
into the ways of God. It is not the speed of our steps
that is important, rather their direction. Gradual
movement *toward* the Father will get you much farther
in the end than will the quick-march tempo of many
legions of Christian foot-soldiers filing in hasty circular
motion around the bootcamp parade grounds of our
faith—but never going anywhere.

Will this be a *practical* book?

There will certainly be a *do* involved—the very
important exercise of learning to relate ourselves to
God the Father in the exciting ways in which Jesus
walked with him and invited us to do likewise. But it
will be a *do* measured not with our hands, fingers, and
feet, but with our brains and hearts.

Before we can *do* rightly we have to learn to *think*
rightly. Above all, we have to learn to think rightly
about God. That is the most vital kind of right

thinking in all the universe. Until that foundation has been laid, nothing else matters, nothing else makes sense.

Once we are thinking correctly, however, many very practical things begin to fall into place. For that reason, I sincerely hope you will look back on this as one of the most practical books you ever read.

Not because you studied it according to some rigid system, or analyzed the three points the author was trying to make in such-and-such a chapter, or took notes, or underlined various passages, or memorized this or that key phrase. Rather, I would hope that the challenging concepts within prompt you to go outside and take some long walks alone, gazing upward toward the mountaintops of your faith, saying, *"O God, teach me to think rightly about you. Help me know you more intimately as my very personal Father!"*

A practical note:

This is a book about God, and he will be referred to in many different ways. Generally the biblical style will be followed; that is, pronouns referring to God (he, him, etc.) will be given in the lowercase, while the words *Father* and *Fatherhood* will appear in uppercase whenever indicating God's Fatherhood. In instances of ambiguity, the uppercase will be employed to clarify that a given reference is to God.

The imaginative portions of what follows, depicting a fictionalized journey and the dialogues that are part of it, are intended to help us break through the one-dimensionalism with which we often approach things of the Spirit. Achieving intimacy with our Father requires learning to live and think on more than one level at a time. Thus, this literary device will be employed, moving us back and forth between the realm of the here and now and the realm of the imagination. The very structure is intended to give you practice in what it "feels" like to be intimate with God your Father.

As deeper intimacy with the Father unfolds within you, seek his voice, not mine, speaking to you.

Finally, write to me, if you are so inclined, and tell me about the hidden things you are discovering about our Father. You may not always hear from me in return, but be assured I will appreciate your words and will bring you before the Father in my own times alone with him.

PROLOGUE:
THE VALLEY AND
THE MOUNTAINS

It was a beautiful land, that high region
obscured by the mist overhead . . . but wild. So
claimed the inhabitants of the valley beneath
the great mountains.

Tales abounded concerning that distant
locale, for from time to time some of the more
intrepid of the valley's residents had ventured
into the foothills, bringing back their reports.

Truly the sun could shine, they said, in those
places where the fog thinned. Its warmth brought
forth from the earth a glorious profusion of
flowers, trees, fragrances, and greenery. Green,
indeed, was everywhere, as if the very color of
growing things produced life itself!

A multitude of viridescent brooks, burns, and creeks chattered downward from high above, clear and inviting. Some said these came from the melting of the previous winter's snow, but no one knew their origins for certain. There was said to be a river even farther up, out of which the smaller rivulets flowed, but no one had ventured high enough to know if such was legend or fact. This river was also said to be turbulent and dangerous, and to think of mounting an expedition in its direction was foolhardy.

Notwithstanding such dangers, folklore held that the meadows, pastures, and forests of the lower hill country seemed to derive their very life from these emerald waters tumbling downward from above, and these lands were unmatched for the varied and delicate shades of color that burst forth each spring. Nowhere did the splendor of the warm months of summer reach greater magnificence. And the fiery arboreal hues of autumn gave peaceful pleasure to any who dared walk the sloped pathways beneath leaves of red, orange, and yellow.

None of the natives of the valley were beguiled, however. The foothills might put on their seasons of gladness, but it was impossible to mistake the ominous nature of the mountains looming above them. Storms could erupt and blizzards blow and thunder rage and avalanches race down upon them without warning. Even asleep, the mountains kept one eye open, and wise mortals who wanted to live a long and natural life kept their distance.

Occasionally valley dwellers ventured into the foothills for a brief glance or two at the scenery, but then quickly scurried back down to the safety and security of their homes in the lowlands.

Yes, the higher regions were beautiful, that could not be denied. Yet better, most sighed wistfully, a life in the secure grayness of the valley than in the uncertain greenery of the foothills beneath the terrifying mountains.

Old musicians and storytellers said a curse had been put upon the whole land, accounting for the fierce wintry displays of its upper sweeps. Others maintained that everything could be explained by natural causes and that only prophets and fools sought deeper meaning in it all.

Indeed, as generations passed, even the mountains themselves became but legends, for the overlying mists grew thick with the passage of the centuries, and in time none of the snowcapped peaks could any longer be seen from the valley floor.

Many of the young philosophers who filled the valley's pulpits and universities maintained that there were no mountains at all, that the tales of their existence were mere myths handed down from an earlier unenlightened era. In time, these new creeds came to govern the prevailing outlook of thought everywhere, even in those fringe regions where the valley terrain penetrated its narrow vales and glens into the surrounding foothills, and thus where, as would be expected, the mountain legends had not died out altogether.

Everyone knew about the Creator-God, of course—the one who had formed the mountains and valley together. Even those who denied the existence of the mountains had not totally forgotten him. In fact, there were frequent revivals of interest in him in various parts of the valley, especially at its edges. But even this did not increase their sense of intimacy with their Creator. For the truth was that the valley inhabitants didn't know much about him . . . or where he lived.

Time passed. The valley grew crowded with cities and churches and industries. Noise and bustle and stress abounded. Technology, electronics, automobiles, television, VCRs, and computers came to dominate the lives of its citizens. The pace of valley life quickened and intensified, while values, character, integrity, and selflessness became outmoded terms. Modernity and sophistication were the prevailing outlook and priority.

One day, however, there appeared in the valley a white-bearded man with astonishing tales to tell.

Not only were the mountains not nearly so fearsome as they all believed, he said, gazing out of clear blue-green eyes, but it was possible to live in them year round. And not merely survive, but live in flourishing abundance! Up there, one might even enjoy a quieter, more peaceful existence than the turmoil that had engulfed the valley.

Nonsense, said the majority of those listening. It could not possibly be. No one could survive winter in the freezing snows that buried the high peaks . . . if such places existed at all.

Ah, he replied, but there were higher places still, above the snows, above the storms, above the frigid wastes. And on those heights could be found meadows and pasturelands where the sun always shone and luxuriant green growth abounded. This was the place of origins, he said, where the emerald rivers flowed for all to drink without measure.

"What!" they exclaimed. "The rivers do not drown you?"

"Drown!" he laughed. "They are rivers of life, not death. Everything up there gives life! Every atom, every molecule, exudes more vitality than any cubic mile down here. The windows of the clear blue vault overhead open to heaven itself! That is why I have come, to lead you there and show you where you may take up residence. There is no reason for anyone to live here in the valley, under these gray fogs.

There is room in that wondrous high country for everyone!"

"No," they said. "We want no part of it."

"But what could possibly keep you here after what I have told you?" he asked.

"We do not believe you. We do not believe there is any such place. And even if there were, it would be impossible to get there. The very notion of being able to climb higher than the snows is absurd. Everyone knows the higher you go, the less oxygen there is and the colder it becomes, until finally all life becomes impossible. We do not know who you are or where you have come from, but you could not have come from above the snows."

"All you have said is true—according to the physics of the valley," he replied. "But in that country, all is different! You cannot apply the valley principles there. Everything operates in reverse. Even the mathematics of that place functions by different rules and equations.

Don't you see what I am telling you? It is a good and pleasant land, where life abounds!"

"The more you say, the more nonsensical it sounds!"

"Do you mean to say you are satisfied with life in the valley?" he asked.

"We are satisfied," they replied.

There was a young man among them, however, who listened eagerly to all the stranger said. His heart longed to know if such regions really existed where a more satisfying life could be found. Whatever other valley inhabitants might say, he had already, though his years were few, begun to find the fogs suffocating and stupefying. In truth, he did not know how much longer he could survive under the cloud of their anesthetizing grayness.

He determined that he would accompany the stranger into the mountains, even if it should cost him the final gasps from his mortal lungs. Better, he reasoned, to die in the quest for life, than to merely subsist in the dull, wearisome gray of the valley.

Not many days thereafter, they set out, the stranger and the young man of the valley who had heard, with eager and hungering heart, the words about life in the mountains above the snows.

None in the valley saw the small expedition leave, nor missed them after they had gone.

———————

The white-bearded stranger never returned to the valley. Indeed, he was quickly forgotten. His own sojourn thereafter took him to the uppermost region of all, but not until he had led the young man to the mountaintops above the snows.

The young man became a scribe of that high country, setting himself to record the stranger's teachings, observations, and stories during their years together in the mountains.

Finally, the day came when he returned to the valley of his origins, hopeful, like the stranger whose footsteps he was now following, of leading others along the upward pathways he himself had trod for more than twenty years.

He came, as the stranger had before him, telling of high regions of life and urging others to take up the quest as he had.

These were the words he spoke to those who clustered about to hear his tale.

———————

PART I
THE INSTINCT TO LOOK UP

———

Gazing from the
Valley toward
the Mountains

1

THE INSTINCT
TO LOOK UP

Gather around, my friends.

Let me tell you of a place I have seen, and of truths I have learned from the lips of one older and wiser than I. He took me from this valley many years ago, when I was younger than many of you. Now I have returned to lead whosoever will come, as I myself was led, out of the valley and into that high region where the sun always shines and winter never comes.

You do not care about leaving the valley, you say.

Ah, but you do!

I know you better than you know yourselves.

Even if we did go, you say, the mountains are too fearsome to contemplate.

I understand. I once stood where you stand now, facing the same fear and reluctance.

And yet I know you, too, long for the lush, green, life-giving high places.

The mountains beckon all of us who live in the valley. Our deepest selves are out of step with the modern life pushing and shoving us on every side.

You recognize the truth of my words, even as you turn away.

For you have caught yourselves glancing upward from time to time, even though the mountains are no longer visible, even though you do not know what it is your eyes seek.

Before the valley philosophers and theologians created the mists with their self-contradictory babblings, there were voices among us calling us to heed that instinctive longing, calling us to hearken once more to the words from former times.

Ah yes, friends, you remember now!

There have been those who have come
among us, summoning us to the mountains.
Come now. Let us seek the faint footprints
left by their memory, that we might follow their
steps up into the regions where we were made
to live.

———————

Deep within *every* mortal heart lies a created hunger for the heavenly mountains of God's presence.

All of us, from our infancy, have silently wondered what lies on the slopes above the mists, hidden from our view . . . up where God dwells.

The animal kingdom comes into existence looking abroad upon the land. Those of the species known as mankind, however, enter life with their gaze directed *upward.*

Lower forms of life are born with *physical* instincts. Their impulses operate *horizontally,* telling them intuitively how to relate to the world around them, to others of their genus, and to different species. Theirs is an instinct toward procreation and survival, toward horizontal relationship and existence.

Man, however, created in the image of God, pos-

sesses instincts of an altogether different nature.
Within us the Creator has implanted *spiritual* instincts, tending far beyond mere physical survival.
Impulses akin to animal instincts surface constantly
within us and are certainly intrinsic to our makeup,
but they remain secondary to the deepest nature of
human personhood.

Man's instinct is *vertical*—a yearning after the high,
the lasting, the eternal. It is an instinct after growth,
after betterment, after significance, after something
and Someone above us. When in touch with the truest
regions of our humanness, we seek the sky, not the
earth.

The lungs of our soul ache to breathe the air of
eternity, and though mists obscure our sight, our deepest perceptions tell us there is more to existence than
that which our physical eyes "see" around us. Something affirms to our innermost being that there are
higher regions where we might live, where the air is
cleaner, where vision is keener, where the senses come
more fully *alive*.

A divine restlessness exists within the hidden
chambers of our soul, stirring us with longings we
cannot identify, and which we futilely attempt to satisfy with bread that is not food, made from husks that
are not grain.

Augustine, that ancient and venerable saint, maintained that our soul is restless until we "find our rest" in him.

Thomas Kelly, that recent and venerable saint, called it "the Light within."

Blaise Pascal, that seventeenth-century defender of the faith, defined it as a God-shaped vacuum, an "infinite abyss," which "can be filled only with an infinite and immutable object . . . God himself."

Hannah Hurnard, that pioneer of mountain byways, wrote of life on the "high places."

And George MacDonald, that nineteenth-century spiritual sage who saw beyond the mists, said, "This is and has been the Father's work from the beginning—to bring us into the home of his heart. This is our destiny."

Why, then, do so few discover the shape of that vacuum in their souls, the illumination of that Light residing within?

Why do we resist the challenge to climb to the mountaintops?

Why is the home of God's heart so remote from where we live out our days? Why do we go to our grave with that destiny, that high calling, unfulfilled?

Why is the human species so at odds with this

inborn instinct of his nature? Allow me to offer three reasons.

One, unlike the animals, man has been given *choice.*

We share instinct with all the animal kingdom, but ours has this difference—we may ignore it. Animals can be no other than they are. Their instinct defines their essence. Not so man. Man may, or may not, follow his instincts, for he has been provided an internal on-off switch that regulates the very centers of his being: the *mind,* where intellect develops; the *heart,* where emotions blossom; and the *soul,* where spiritual sensitivities ripen.

This switch, which controls each of the above, is located in that most decisive of regions: the *will.*

This switch is called *choice.*

The degree to which man *chooses* to follow his God-hungry instinct will determine the extent to which mind, heart, soul, and will reach their fullness of maturity and potential, and whether they operate with unity and harmony inside him.

Two, many factors of modern society work strenuously to dull the inner Voice that speaks of the Light, calling us toward that true and only destination where our mind, heart, soul, and will can find rest, peace, and totality of being.

Contemporary society and our practical peers of modernism tell us "there is nothing out there." We may gaze upward all we want, they say, but we will find nothing but blue emptiness. There are no heavenly peaks surrounding this valley where man must dwell.

Indeed, they say, we must look *within* if we would discover the significance we seek. *Man himself* is the emphatic and only center of the universe.

Three, sin, as intrinsic to the human disposition as the intuitive upward bent of our inner sight, declares, as it has since the days of the Garden, that there is no one to whom we *must* look up, no one to whom we *owe* allegiance. This lie from sin's smooth lips grates contrary to our deepest being, yet is one our lower nature eagerly receives.

Just the opposite, says the enemy: *You,* and no one else, are the sole master of your fate. *No one* has the right to exact obedience from you. You have *no need* of any Other. There exists *no injunction to bow* before a God, a Creator, a Lord.

This lie is *independence,* and it comes from the lowest bowels of the earth, not the high realms of the heavenly mountains.

Instinct calls us upward. *The lie* forces our gaze downward.

In believing it, we fight against our very self.

Choice, modernism, and sin prevent us from apprehending our destiny and keep us from the destination and mountaintop sanctuary wherein we were made to dwell.

2

MODERNISM
RESENTS
FATHERHOOD

Ah, my friends, does not your heart leap at the very thought of a home for your innermost spirit, sheltered from the anxieties that press upon you daily? Do not your legs itch to climb instead of forever walking in circles on the valley floor? Do not your lungs ache to rid themselves of the cloying gray smog and breathe the clean, fresh, alpine air?

Do you not think that if only the mountains were not so dreadfully terrifying, you might agree to venture there with me?

Listen to me, friends. Put away, if only for a brief interlude, the press of today's schedule, waiting even now to invade with its urgencies. Keep it at bay a minute or two longer.

Lay aside worries of what friends and colleagues, even your family, would think if they knew you were reflecting upon the "unpracticalities" of your spiritual core. No one else need know for the present.

Cast off the cloak of reservation that has prevented you from examining the corners of disquiet deep within, corners that even you have been reluctant to identify.

Do you not, in this quiet moment, long for relief from the restlessness and frustration with which life seems filled? Would you not rejoice to find that you might walk away from them and enter into a locale of calm, where the intensities and annoyances of today's frantic and uncertain pace lose their power to make you tense and anxious?

I know of just such a place. I have seen it, friends, and am here to show you the way! Let me lead you to the waters of a deep, quiet pool, whose calm surface the pressuring stones of life cannot disturb. Does not the very thought of such a place cause you to sigh with longing thirst, "Ah, could such truly be possible . . . for me? Could such waters quench every thirst of my mind, my heart, my soul—refreshing and cold and invigorating, always renewing, never running dry? Could they fill the emptiness, as a great cavern within me, that I often feel?"

Yes, dear friend! The place from which such waters bubble forth is neither unattainable nor distant. To reach it will take a climb, it is true, and you may find the way strenuous at times. It is no quest for the faint of heart.

Up there, in the mountains, waters stream forth from divine springs. It only remains for you to find the source of those headwaters and then bend down and drink, quenching your thirst with those clean, life-giving streams.

These mountain waters of the spirit gush forth out of their emerald source with such divine power and force that there is thirst-quenching élan vital sufficient for every being upon the earth. They narrow and lose their potency, however, the farther into the valley of man's self-sufficiency they descend, becoming at the bottom but scant tributaries of drizzle—enough to keep the valley inhabitants alive, but without the energy with which they were intended to thrive.

But up high, at the Source, exist waters aplenty with which to fill that empty cistern within your soul!

———————

The instant you begin to pack your bags in anticipation of the journey upward out of the valley, you are bombarded with all manner of reservations.

"Be practical," say a thousand voices at once. "Life is to be lived in the here and now. Whoever said we were supposed to be saints? You don't want to turn into a nun, a preacher, a monk, for heaven's sake! Get real, man. People will think you're a nut if they know you're thinking about *this* kind of stuff."

Multitudinous and persistent will be the bombarding objections, even from your Christian friends living their Christian valley lives.

All your training, all of what you consider the "practical experience" of your life, all your concerns over that most harmless demon called "what other people might think," all the observations of your friends and acquaintances and how *they* live their lives down here in the low places, all your anxieties about turning into a stuffy cleric . . . all these will bring their arguments to bear against you in denial of the Voice calling you to look upward and inward. Forget about it, they will tell you, and "get on" with *real* life.

Yet their arguments collide with disconsonance against that instinct you cannot hide from, that *you-est* part of you—the urge that says there *is* more than these so-called practicalities would admit.

The collision between sky-gazing intuition and earthbound reasoning knocks us about. Confusion assaults us, exacerbated all the more when we mention *fatherhood* as being the source of this higher destination we seek, the source of the high-mountain spring itself. For the word "father" has become odious to modern ears.

Attempting to disrupt the inner summons from on high, discrepant voices pressure and persuade us to reject the concept of fatherhood in three of its essential attributes:

—its authority,

—its masculinity,

—its Godness.

An enshrouding cloud has settled over the valley, graying and obfuscating vision of the mountains by blocking the truths inherent in authority, masculinity, and Godness and, thus, assuring our rebellion against these three inherent elements of fatherhood.

By our own *choice* we revolt against the very notion of someone other than ourselves in AUTHORITY.

Modern society, at every turn, prevails upon us with a thousand subtleties to reject MASCULINITY.

And the *sin* to which man succumbs draws us into the lie of independence, persuading us there is no GOD to whom we owe allegiance.

Fatherhood as we have traditionally known it, say all three, is an outmoded convention from some archaic era. Times have changed, and so must our approach to this mythical thing our unenlightened predecessors called by such an oppressive name. We will keep the term, but it must be utterly redefined. It must be stripped of its authority, de-masculinized, and humanized. Only then will it be unthreatening enough to suit us.

Those previously existing under the weight of its authority must be given rights of cosignificant status so that no one rules *over* any other. In this enlightened age, no child or woman should feel lesser in rank.

Its masculinity must be given an equal injection of feminism. The genders will then be equipotent in stature.

Moreover, the Fatherhood of God must be irrevocably rejected for the illusionary absurdity it always was. It is to God's *Person*ness we must look, giving femininity and motherhood their equal share with the former bias of *His*ness.

Thus, these valley corruptions of antifatherhood enter our perceptions at all levels, carrying out their cancerous work, eating away the very marrow of our spiritual fiber.

Antifatherhood is no benign cancer; it is the fatal malignancy of modernism. Its curse cannot be escaped. Its deadly molecules swirl about in the very air we breathe, and *none* is immune. Nor can its cells be isolated to a few remote and inconsequential regions within us where they can be "tolerated."

Antifatherhood is positively lethal, and if allowed to take hold and grow, it will infect mind, heart, soul, and will with its poison. It deadens those unfamiliar with the way of God to the very instinct that can lead them out of the quagmire of their despair, disquiet, and frustration. It prevents those acquainted with God's work from laying hold of the fullness of their childship because of their antipathy toward fatherhood. Ultimately it will kill the ability to *think* accurately, to *feel* appropriately, to *grow* maturely, and to *choose* wisely.

It is in that region where spiritual sensitivities sprout and grow—the soul—that the death from this antifatherhood cancer comes first. Not spiritual death—what the Bible calls eternal death, damnation. Rather, it is death to the capacity to respond correctly to the One calling to us from on high.

If you would take up the quest to find those satisfying waters that can fill the inner places, if you would lay hold of that unknown Something calling you to reach higher than you previously have, the first step of preparation is this: *to lay aside whatever may predispose you to respond negatively to authority, to masculinity, and to God himself,* whether that be background, experiences, training, tendencies of prior reactions, or teachings of modernism you have adopted as your own.

Now is neither the time nor the place to argue or explain *why* you must do so, or to debate modernity's corrupted frame of reference. Perhaps such will be appropriate another time in another setting. For now, however, you simply must lay them aside.

The malignant fog of all our previous biases has to be left behind if we are going to journey out of the valley together and embark upon the upward path toward Fatherhood.

3

WHAT DOES
FATHER MEAN?

Walk outside. Look up. Yes, there are
mountains up there, hidden by the valley mists,
calling to be explored.

Can you not hear them, even in their silence,
summoning you, inviting you, beckoning you
with the words: "Come . . . life is here!"

Behind that haze, among the peaks, there is
water to be drunk, air to be breathed, wondrous
sights to be relished. There also exists,
surrounding the Fountainhead of the heavenly
spring, a mansion, a place to dwell, beside which
every house in the valley is but a straw hovel.

There is a rumor about that anyone may take
up residence inside it.

It is more than a rumor, my friends. It is truth itself!

Breathe deeply as you gaze upward. Do not the high places of possibility beckon you? Might not that great high-country manor be the very place you have always dreamed of living?

Breathe in to the capacity of your lungs once again, then exhale slowly. Gaze upward a few seconds more.

Does not some inner voice tell you that already you have taken a step closer to the One who is out there? Do you not long to know his purpose? Where he might be wanting to take you?

Can you not sense, in some way you cannot describe, that even in doing so you have touched reality on a new level, where you have never been before this day?

Our destiny calls us. The odyssey is mountainward.

The mansion where that Presence dwells lies among those lofty mountains, whose slopes you descry but whose peaks are yet enshrouded in unknowing and uncertainty.

Come with me!

Let us venture into those regions, climbing out and above the fogs of this valley, where we have spent far too long.

The Father desires to lead us to the high places, to fill our empty reservoirs with the waters of his being.

He would have us find that home among the mountains that are his heart, and make it our abode.

———

In the spiritual awakening that has taken place within Christendom during the last three decades, it has become customary to regard the least understood aspect of the Godhead as the Holy Spirit.

A great revival has swept through the land, reintroducing this shadowy third member of the Trinity in a widespread way.

Underlying this renaissance of Christianity's vibrancy is the foundational assumption that those calling themselves Christians are well acquainted with the Father and Son facets of God's being.

It may be, however, that the least apprehended of God's triune personalities is his Fatherhood. Having been taken for granted, the knowing of God the Father has receded into the background behind a relationship with the Son and an intimacy with the Holy Spirit.

Christians speak of "walking with Jesus." Evangelicals regard salvation as based on "a personal relationship with Jesus Christ." Charismatics credit a great deal of God's activity in their lives and ministries and churches to "the work of the Holy Spirit."

Furthermore, it has come to be assumed that we cannot know the Father with intimacy or personal immediacy, which is the reason God sent Son and Spirit.

Of all the falsehoods perpetuated by the theologies of men, this must surely be one of the most heartbreaking to God himself. For *it is his Father's heart he desires us to know most of all!* This is where intimacy of relationship begins. The Fatherness of God provides the very foundation for both other aspects of his divine nature. Without Fatherhood there could be neither Son nor Spirit.

———————

When we say "God is our Father," what do we mean?

Is *Father* merely a term of procreation, of begetting? Is *creating* all there is to this Fatherhood? Does our relationship to this being we cannot see extend no further than birth—both the physical and the spiritual?

Alas, we live (exercising minds, hearts, souls, and wills) as if such is indeed the case. We resemble ungrateful children who grab a gift but then turn their backs and walk away, never expressing thanks, never even acknowledging whence the gift originated.

All men and women take *physical* life, but most offer nothing back in response to their Maker. Most do not even view it as a gift at all but as a mere fact of the natural world.

Those numbering themselves Christians receive *spiritual* life and give back perhaps a little more, but chiefly to the Son and Spirit. They pay only cursory heed to him out of whom both flow—the One who sustains that life of second birth they enjoy.

Thus, by lives lived virtually independent of him—on both physical and spiritual planes—is verified the nonunderstanding we bring to the very idea of *Father*.

Why do we bustle about in our spiritual abodes, on a first-name and familiar basis with brothers and sisters, Son and Spirit, yet think so little of the Householder himself? Why do we regard him with a detachment that relegates him to the attic regions, leaving him uninvolved in the daily goings-on of the very place of which he is the Master?

Why, I ask?

Because we find it comfortable to do so.

Whatever the Son may have told us, we can't help being just a little afraid of the Father. We haven't yet learned what manner of Father he is.

Jesus invites us to fellowship with him and walk beside him. He has given commands to be followed, it is true, but he will not press the issue. Jesus says, "I obey my Father," but he will not force us to do the same. He shows us his example, but leaves us free to choose.

The crowds came, the crowds went. The rich young ruler came, then left. Jesus did not try to convince him to change his mind. His own best friends stumbled and occasionally fell away. Yet Jesus did not coerce. He went about his business, leaving the on-off switch of their wills fully operative.

The Holy Spirit, meanwhile, is the "feel-good" third of God's being. He will pray for us when we don't know what to pray. He guides us. He gives us gifts. He inspires us. He leads us into truth. Jesus called him the Comforter, and that is what he does: He soothes and consoles.

But for those few who do venture, not just two-thirds of the way into God's house, but *all* the way, through the Son and Spirit, up toward the mountaintops and into the *Father's* presence, the parameters of relationship between Creator and created take on huge added weight.

The words of the Father are more exacting. He says: "My son showed you his example . . . now you *must* obey. He left you room . . . I will leave you none."

He says: "When I send you my Spirit, he may give you of my pleasing gifts. But this is only to enable you to give your life wholly to *me*. The gifts I, as Father, give are all good, and are even richer and more complete than what he showed you. But to receive them fully, I may require of you the cross."

There is no compromise, no half-measure with God's Fatherhood. Little wonder, then, that we try to keep Fatherhood at arm's length, locked away in the attic of our spiritual house.

Yet Jesus himself spoke of the importance of knowing the Father. "I must be about My Father's business," he said. And later: "I and the Father are one."

Endless, indeed, *is* the fellowship . . . unlimited *is* the comfort . . . wondrous *is* the love to which the Son and the Spirit attest—but only when we know the Father aright.

It is into this *knowing* that Jesus came to lead and instruct us.

He seeks to introduce us to a life lived *with* the Father. Not a mere begetting, but a life of ongoing, moment-by-moment intimacy on all levels of humanhood—mind, heart, soul, and will.

It is toward intimacy with the Father that the Son would guide us. For such he was born. For such he died.

If we do not take his hand and walk along the upward pathway the Son has marked out for us, following in his footsteps, we will only be "offspring" of the Father—children *begotten,* but not sons and daughters of *intimacy.*

Let us, therefore, as Thomas Kelly exhorted, "dare to venture together into the inner sanctuary of the soul, where God meets man in awful intimacy."

Do not shrink away from that word, for truly the association He seeks is not "awful." Invert the syllables—full of awe—and discover the key to the great doorway of life, the pathway upward out of the valley!

The fear of the Lord is the beginning of wisdom, says Proverbs.

What is this fear? Mortal terror of something awful?

A thousand times no!

Rather, it is an openhearted bowing before the *awe-full*—a God *full* of *awe* and mystery and wonder.

Does he truly want to be *my* Father and spend time with *me* and see to *my* every need, *my* every thought? Does he want to take care of *me* and reveal himself to *me?*

Does he want to fill all my *mind* can think, all my *heart* feels, all my *soul* invisibly longs for, and transform my *will* into the most powerful instrument available for the doing of good?

Does he want to give me his business to be about, just like Jesus?

Yes, all this and more awaits us. Of such *is* life on the mountaintops.

Ah, my heart cannot contain the hugeness of such astounding possibilities!

The God of the universe, the Creator of the heavens and the earth, the Father of Jesus Christ himself desires daily companionship with *me!*

He wants me to call him Father!

4
WHO IS THE FATHER?

I see you are listening closely, my friends, intrigued by my tale. Before we set out for the high places, however, take heed. The longer you have been breathing the fogs of this lower region, the more difficult it will be to fill your lungs with the cleaner air above. The longer your eyes have been blurred by the cloudy mists, the harder it will be to see the blue vaults of the wide spaces of heaven above.

It will not be easy, but we must learn to breathe deeply and to refocus our eyes. And how wondrously the journey will be worth it.

———————

Christians and non-Christians, atheists and agnostics,

theologians and laymen, thinkers and nonthinkers, pastors and priests, men and women and children alike possess but hazy and scant images of the sort of being God the Father actually is.

What is his being, his character, his nature? What are his essential purposes in his dealings with man? Who *is* God?

Men and women have been asking variations of this question since time began. Yet because it is so lofty an inquiry, they bring a series of devastating misconceptions to it.

Most of us can parrot phrases and principles we have been taught. Theologians and writers, priests and preachers, lecturers and conference leaders till and retill the same tired soil of their worn-out doctrines, offering little more than what *they* have been taught. But few really *know* the nature of he with whom Jesus went out into the hills alone.

Incredibly, we are even afraid to inquire. Somehow we have gotten the notion that God does not want us asking too many questions about him.

What mother or father would scold an inquisitive child for the question: "Mommy, Daddy . . . what are you like? I want to know you more deeply." What joy would fill the heart of the parent hearing such words!

But the keepers of the ecclesiastical doorways tell

us *not* to question, *not* to probe, *not* to inquire too deeply into God's character. Hungry hearts and active brains threaten their established systems.

Salvation is not at issue here. A prisoner sitting in a stone cell may receive food every day from a warden he never sees. The food nourishes him and offers him life, though he knows nothing of the hand providing it. And if one day a writ of pardon comes from the hand of a forgiving and gracious judge, the prisoner will be unshackled and full of rejoicing when he walks outside into the air of freedom, though he has never laid eyes on his savior and knows nothing about him.

Likewise, salvation comes through Jesus Christ to millions for whom relationship with the Son thereafter is very near and real and personal . . . yet who may never meet his Father face-to-face, nor seek to know what manner of Father Jesus repeatedly spoke of.

It is possible—indeed, even likely—to enter into the second birth made available by God's Spirit . . . yet exist in only a textbook relationship with his Father-hood.

These Christians are part of God's family, and they have established a certain level of relationship with Son and Spirit. Such men and women may evidence genuine spiritual life. With respect to the Father, however, they have a relationship we might describe as "knowing a friend of a friend."

The relationship is one of vague familiarity, not intimacy. Even after years as members of his family, it is possible to know very little about the nature of the Father Jesus so intimately called *Abba*.

We relate to the Father as to the two bookends framing existence. We recognize him as the vague begetting source of life—the Alpha; and we tremble when we think of him as the severe and terrible judge of sin on the great white throne of eternity—the Omega. Between the two, however, most live out their lives largely inattentive to that deepest fundamental relationship between child and Father from which they were created to draw every breath. Life between the bookends offers a comfortable and pleasant, social and churchy, spiritual existence, leaving the fulfillment of the larger and all-important purposes of the Father for the next life.

Such is not the kind of life into which Jesus invited his disciples when he said, "Follow me." It is not the kind of life he lived for—and died for. *Full* fellowship—the "whole measure" of spiritual maturity of which Paul spoke—the "full gospel" Jesus came to reveal, is *fellowship with his Father.*

To move toward intimacy with the Father, therefore, requires that we acknowledge the following with honesty and humble self-examination: It is easier than we may have realized to know a great deal "about" the Father without knowing *him* personally.

What is the Father like? This is *the* most important question of our existence; it is *the* universal quest. Finding the answer and forming a proper response to that answer is the ultimate journey upon which our earthly footsteps are bound, the pilgrimage toward our destiny as human beings.

5

THE DIFFICULTY
OF INTIMACY

The moment we embark toward the
mountains from out of the valley, one of the
first things we will notice is that the way
contains difficulties, even treacherous cliffs and
rifts we must somehow get across, but which
look like they will kill us if we try.

It seems impossible at first, nothing like the
beauties I have been promising. You may find
yourself losing sight of the mountains altogether
and think you shall never reach their heights,
which grow more obscure than ever.

But faint not.

Though these chasms and canyons have long
separated the mountain travelers from the valley

dwellers, their rocky slopes are temporary, and, once traversed, the higher way becomes a delight to walk.

To guide us we will have the footsteps of One who has gone this way before. Though the track is stained with his blood, there is no danger. He has marked it out with his footprints for us to follow.

His way will lead us upward, across the chasms, until we draw within sight of the regions we seek.

Why *is* Fatherhood obscure?

Primarily, of course, because God's holiness and infinitude cannot coexist with the selfish and finite nature of humankind. The Israelites of old could not look upon the face of God lest they die. Moses could not even wear sandals in the presence of God.

There sits a natural and intrinsic gulf between God's Fatherhood and man's humanness—a great distance, a chasm of unlikeness.

That being the case, then, how can we know him intimately?

How? Through the Son. God sent the Son that we might see in a man what we could not otherwise behold.

The same chasm doesn't exist between Jesus and ourselves.

He was one of us. He lived, he breathed, he spoke, he ate, he became tired and frustrated, he slept, he experienced relationships, he had good friends, he had friends who turned against him. We can read words that actually fell from his lips. His being, his personality, his humanness are graspable.

And Jesus came to tell us: *"The Father is just like me."*

Even though Jesus said the Father and Son were one, even though he told his disciples, "If you have seen me, you have seen the Father," even though he points consistently and *only* to the Father . . . the Father still remains distant and obscure.

Why?

If we take Jesus at his word, we see that it is the *Father* we are to worship, it is the *Father* whom we are to seek to know, it is the *Father* whose work we are to be about, it is the *Father* with whom we are to walk in

close and daily and constant friendship and relationship . . . as Jesus himself did.

Thus exists the great dichotomy: God the Father is
holy and infinite; we are sinful and finite. We are
separate from him. He is invisible to human eyes. He
does not speak with audible words. No man but Moses
has seen his face. His footprints mark no *place* upon
the earth. In all finite human ways of "knowing," God
the Father is unknowable. *Yet only in knowing him do
we live as he purposed us to live.*

Therein lies the mystery of God's Fatherhood.

Words we are all familiar with and have heard from
the days of our spiritual infancy will immediately
spring to mind in "explanation" of this phenomenon
that lies at the core of the Christian message. Words
such as "Jesus bridged the gap" . . . "Through the
Cross we come back into fellowship with God" . . .
"Christ atoned for our sins" . . . "Jesus reconciles us to
God" . . . "Jesus Christ is our mediator, making peace
between God and sinful man."

True enough every one—and thank God! Thank
God for making provision in the midst of a doomful
dilemma of eternal proportions that we could never
have overcome ourselves.

These explain the underpinnings that are the foundation of the Christian faith. They clarify why salva-

tion is possible and why those appropriating their truths no longer walk under the inevitable curse of sin.

Again we rejoice and say, *Thank God* for these truths!

Salvation has come. Fellowship with Christ has come. The Christian's eternal "position" vis-à-vis the Father is secure.

But, alas, such explanations are chiefly theological. For most—I do not say all—who call themselves Christians, and certainly for all who do not, they accomplish little in an intensely practical way to lead into that daily, moment-by-moment, walking-and-talking, child-with-Father intimacy. We stop short of the very thing Jesus said was his deepest heart's desire—that we know his Father as he did.

We are saved, but we still don't walk with a consciousness that our hand is snugly resting in the Father's.

Intimacy—it's hard to come by.

6

LOOKING UPWARD

Starting out from the secure doctrinal homes in the valley you have known so long can be more than a little fearful. The first steps are often timid ones.

Though fear of the Lord is the beginning of wisdom, we're often so fogged in by the traditions of men that we can't move beyond them to find out what the Lord's wisdom actually might be. Especially dubious are we of any so-called new doctrine that seeks to explain things in ways we're unaccustomed to.

And now I have come to the valley talking about new and fresh ways of "knowing" God, challenging you to travel up into the mountain

regions you cannot even see from here. I would
be surprised if there wasn't some quivering in
your spiritual knees.

Truly I understand, dear friends. I myself
lived in the valley for many years before
following the white-bearded man into the
mountain regions.

How well I recall my own first tentative steps!

How afraid I was that I might overstep the
traditional bounds of my Christian training in
leaving the comfort of the valley terrain I knew
so well.

Oh, but I soon learned to trust the stranger,
my guide and mentor who soon became my
friend. I saw that he desired only to lead me *to*
God my Father, not away from him. How
reassuring it was also to realize that he was only
following his own Master's footsteps and
showing me what there was to learn along the
way.

Likewise, as we now leave the valley and

journey upward together, I only desire to lead you along some of the lesser-known pathways where the footsteps of Jesus himself have led.

Jesus sought his Father alone in the hills, and he invites us to do the same as we accompany him upward.

If you cannot altogether leave your timidity, at least do not let it detain you.

In time you will look back and realize that your fears have vanished altogether in the fresh lofty air of the spirit.

Come . . . the adventure begins!

Quiet yourself just now.

Put away pen that would underline, take notes, or scribble thoughts in the margin.

We have arrived at the edge of the valley. The first step along the upward path awaits us. We begin now to move toward a new realm of "getting to know" our Father.

Pray with me, will you.

Father of Jesus, God of the universe, perhaps I have not known you as intimately as you would like. It matters not the cause. This moment has come in my life when I have become aware that I want to know you with the kind of intimacy that your Son, Jesus, knew you. I want to walk and fellowship and communicate and interact with you in a close and daily way. I want to know you fully, or at least as fully as is possible. But with the recognition that I don't know you as well as I want to comes the realization that I don't know how to get to know you.

*So I ask you to help me. I **want** to know you, and to do so, I need your help and guidance. I open my mind and my heart and my soul to you, and I ask you to begin turning them in new directions— toward all that your Fatherhood would speak into the depths of my being. Begin strengthening my will, too, so that it becomes trained in pointing the way you, as my Father, would have me go. Help me to think, to feel, and to choose in harmony with your Fatherhood in my life.*

*Reveal yourself to me. Show me what you are like, show me your nature and your character. Open me to **all** you would make known to me about yourself. Teach me to call you Father.*

Now, please set down this book, close your eyes, and pray this prayer again. Do not repeat the words written on these pages, but pray quietly in your own words, giving to the Father the open and humble expression of your *own* heart.

This is a prayer any man, woman, or child can pray, whatever their level of spiritual development.

To all who open themselves and humbly ask for the Father to make himself known, worlds of *true knowing* will slowly and gently begin to open. Not because of any how-to lists you will learn of here, but from being in the presence of the Father.

By continuing to pray your own version of this prayer daily, bringing it to every step of the way we progress together as well as to the Scriptures you read, you will find yourself gradually perceiving truths on newer and deeper levels, at the most unexpected times and places. This will be the Father speaking to you. He always answers prayer! If you speak the words in earnest to him, you can be sure he *will* give answers to your heart and mind.

Not all at once. In fact, no change may be apparent for hours, days, maybe even years. But as the desires of your prayers are infused into all of you, the Father will answer them. Such prayers *will* open doors and windows into the higher realms of the Father's being and purposes.

With every new step we take on this journey, silently lift up to God the heart-opening reaffirmation: *Reveal truth to me. Show me how to call you Father. Draw me into your presence.*

Do you seek practicalities?

You have just prayed the most vital and practical prayer in all the universe—the prayer God longs to hear his creatures pray.

With those sixteen simple words, you have begun a quest that will change the course of your spiritual life! And as long as you continue to orient your inner being Father-ward, it is a quest that will continue to lead you to new heights, which will, in turn, open into realms of new depths of "knowing" throughout this life . . . and throughout eternity.

We are now embarking on a journey to discover he whom it delighted Jesus' heart to seek. This journey, upon which the Son invites us, is a quest of discovery. He bids us rise with him early, a long while before day, while the world yet sleeps. He invites us to accompany him into the quiet hills alone. As our Guide and Friend and elder Brother, he bids us toward the mountains, there to discover intimacy with his Father . . . and ours.

PART II
HIDDEN
SECRETS ABOUT
OUR MAKER

———

Beginning the

Climb Upward

7
GETTING
TO KNOW

Where are you now . . . at this very moment?

Riding a bus home from work? Snatching a few minutes during your lunch hour or between classes? Trying to squeeze in a few minutes of quiet reading before your next appointment or before the children get home from school?

Most of you sojourning with me are busy and hurried people, for whom even finding the time to attend thoughtfully to these words is a chore.

Do your valley duties press too closely to allow you to concentrate as you read? Sit down, even for a few seconds. Close your eyes and breathe in deeply. This upward journey toward the mountains cannot be taken unless you are

willing and able to distance yourself inwardly
and mentally from the normal and hectic valley
pace.

We're attempting to discover a new way to
live. Therefore, you're going to have to find a
place inside yourself, a quiet little corner, where
the urgent pace cannot intrude. Keep about
your affairs, but in the midst of them find a
calm center inside you. Such regions can always
be discovered, if we take the time to search them
out and then practice moving in and out of
these divinely quiet centers, back and forth
amid our day's activities.

Discovering Fatherhood, you see, is as much
a process of discovering about yourself as it is
discovering about God.

We are not accustomed to living in this "quiet
center of the soul," and doing so takes practice
and concentration. But that is where the
journey into the mountains must be made—in a
solitary corner of being where, for however long

each day, you allow no one entrance but the Spirit of God alone, as he leads you upward toward the Father.

So, my friends, it is time now to leave the valley behind and begin our expedition in earnest.

As we go, let us together spend time leisurely, being in no hurry about the process of getting to know him, fretting not over what the world might call practicalities, leaving behind the fog-imbued compulsion toward the accumulation of mere knowledge, and instead cultivating intimacy with him . . . learning truly and rightly to know him.

———

What is *knowing?*

Two ways of knowing exist, do they not? We say that we "know" things, and we say that we "know" people.

The former refers to *information* you possess. You say you know facts and data concerning the multiplication table, the discovery of America, or the content of the book of Ephesians. This is knowledge of an intellectual sort, most of which you have been taught. There needs be no particular emotional connection with such knowing. It merely exists as raw data in your brain.

People, on the other hand, are known not through brain cells, but by an emotive connection that draws you into fellowship. Bonds, shared interests, common goals, similar outlooks, mutual admiration, time spent together interacting on many levels about many things—these and a hundred other subtleties draw individuals together into the kind of relationship that eventually results in the phrase, "I *know* you . . . and I recognize that you *know* me."

The first kind of knowing is learned. It can, though doesn't always, come instantaneously. It is often, though not always, taught.

The second comes through interaction. It *never* comes instantaneously. It *cannot* be taught. I can't know you by reading a book about you. I know you by getting to know *you*.

This unfortunate use of the same word for two very distinctive phenomena leads to a great deal of confusion in our attempt to "know" God.

We read, we study, we are taught, we probe the Scriptures, we discuss, we listen to the declarations of pastors, speakers, teachers, and authors, gaining a wealth of useful and often biblically correct information. What we assemble in the process, however, is a mere informational matrix of knowledge of the first sort. It is something like putting together a mathematical chart, into whose boxes we gather what data we can learn about God. When enough of the chart is filled in, we begin to conclude that we *know* God.

If I want to know *you,* however, I cannot do so by compiling a data spreadsheet of your characteristics. I can't "learn" you . . . I must "get to know" you. I must spend time with you; I must cultivate bonds of relationship with you.

The Germans, precise and ordered people that they are, have three different words to distinguish the different ways of "knowing."

Wissen is to know information, to be informed about a certain matter. It indicates the possession of factual knowledge.

Kennen is to know a *person.*

Kennenlernen—literally, "to learn to know"—describes the intermediary act of *getting to know* an individual. This compound word reveals an interconnection between the two ways of knowing, pointing out the essential, qualitative *process* involved.

The question before each one of us, therefore,

becomes: Into which category does our "knowledge" of God the Father fall—the *informational* or the *intimate?*

Which brings us to another important question: What manner of "knowing" do you seek?

No judgment will be passed upon those seeking informative, factual knowledge. Such is a useful and necessary component of spiritual life.

However, since such will not be the focus here, those desirous of accumulating data with which to fill in the charts and tables of their *Wissen* regarding God's Fatherhood will no doubt find this a most unpractical journey. We are taking no notebooks with us, only stout climbing shoes.

There will be little to write down as we progress, no how-to lists of steps toward increased spirituality, no keys to self-analysis and fulfillment, few gems to jot in the margins of your reference Bibles, little into which to sink the teeth of your theological intellects. You may listen to my every word and conclude, "There is nothing here, only vague unpracticalities."

Kennen—not *Wissen*—is the object of our pursuit, through the process of *kennenlernen.*

Kennenlernen does not come through lists and notes, nor through what the modernity of the valley world deems "practicalities," nor through anecdotal or humorous examples of this truth or that. No informational matrix, no cognitive analysis, no cerebral dissection of this book or even the Scriptures can open the door that will enable us to "get to know" the Father.

To do that, we must move upward into his presence.

For those whose hearts are open to what he reveals to them, what more practical experience could there be in all the world?

For those seeking *Wissen* only, however, such a quest will seem vague, distant, and meaningless. Perhaps the time for it will be better suited to a later season of life when the thirst-quenching properties of the *Wissen* they have stored up through the years begin to run dry.

8

SECRETS ABOUT OUR MAKER

Our journey involves little more than one thing: cultivating the kind of vision Jesus spoke of when he said, "Behold!" We're climbing up out of the fogs of the lowland so as to uncloud our eyes that we might be capable of beholding the face of our Father.

As the valley fades into the mist behind us, you will find yourself centering down into that quiet place within you. You are discovering already that you can retreat there at any time. It takes but an instant's remembrance, and suddenly you are there . . . with your Master, your hand in his, following him along the high pathways.

Throughout the day, as you begin practicing this conscious inner retreat to your quiet center, cultivating the habit of living in the sanctuary you share only with your Lord, while simultaneously going on about the duties (perhaps even fast-paced ones) of your daily life, you will gradually discover your spiritual eyes growing more keen.

Practice, therefore, seeing the fingerprints of the Father about you. This is the first lesson of the low hills, and that by which the mountains above become increasingly visible.

———————

Beginning our journey into the hills with a prayer, asking for God to reveal truth to us, is the only appropriate starting point. Indeed, by *no* other means than the Father's revelation can truth come. Nothing merely *said* here will open truth to your inner ears.

As you prayed in chapter 6, tiptoeing gingerly into that silent chamber within your heart where dwells the Spirit of God, did everything previously abstract about his Fatherhood suddenly become clarified in your mind?

Of course not.

Kennenlernen takes time.

God answers prayer, and there are few prayers he is more anxious to answer than that one. But he is in no hurry. God's purposes cannot be rushed. He *will* answer your heart's desire, but quietly and in his own chosen manner and time.

Nor will revelation come primarily in the region of your brain. He will reveal himself to your heart when, and in quietly subtle ways, you least expect.

How do we then begin to enter into those still, quiet, heart regions where revelation comes?

By training ourselves to look *inside,* into the "heart" of those things God has made. There is the first place the Fatherhood of God begins to come into focus, for we begin to "get to know" him by looking for his character and personality within his created universe.

God created the universe full of secrets, mysteries, and dichotomies.

Without exaggeration, we can say that in all things there are multiple levels at which they can be seen and understood.

Everything!

In the physical creation, in scriptural truths, in the animal kingdom, in human relationships . . . everywhere there are *surface* appearances that contain *subsurface* meanings, implications, and significance.

Learning to look into those hidden, secret meanings gives us the eyes necessary to begin beholding our Father.

With the eyes one may cast his gaze upon a tree and perceive a trunk enclosed with hard bark, to all appearances stiff and dead and lifeless. But deep inside, the secret of life itself flows through the fibrous growing stuff. Ah, the mysteries contained within that wood!

Deep below, in the earth, where all is dark and wet, roots draw nourishment from the soil, through an osmosis no one completely understands, and pull those needful nutrients from out of the ground, through the flow of sap, up between the majestic trunk and its bark, out through the branches, where at length is produced leaves, buds, and tender shoots of new growth. The leaves in turn point their green faces to the sun and drink from its rays to bring life into the tree from the sky, mirroring above the ground the activity of the roots below.

What a symphony of natural miracles at work in perfect, silent, invisible harmony!

The sun communicates with the black interior of the earth, the clouds send rain from the sky to moisten the soil—all these wonders of nature function in marvelous unity of purpose and life. What no thousand geniuses together could create in a laboratory—the miracle of life—flourishes in grand profusion all around us every instant, from each blade of grass the foot steps on, to the mightiest oak or redwood.

It is possible, however, never to behold even a hint of all this.

Many never do.

For the mysteries of life are *hidden*.

One can walk through a forest without apprehending the miracles at work beneath the bark that surrounds the trunks, underfoot in the ground, in the leaves waving in the sunny breezes.

The mysteries exist, none would question that. The question is—who sees them?

It is fearfully easy *not* to see. It is possible to wander through the day utterly oblivious to the hidden secrets of life so close they touch us on every level.

When one holds a bright, perfect, fragrant rose in his hand, well opened and lush, who cannot marvel at the spectacular display of God's creative hand?

Why do we admire the rose? Is it for the spectacular colors and pleasant aroma? Are these bright petals what we would call the *glory* of the rosebush?

Of course.

But the rose has deeper truths to tell . . . *if* we have the kind of eyes Jesus told us to develop—the kind of eyes that see below and into and *inside.*

What deeper truths?

Truths about the One who made it!

The *true* glories of the rose speak their deepest messages at a far more inner level . . . their mysteries . . . their secrets . . . the glimpses they give us of eternal things . . . the glimpses they give us of the Father.

Have you ever held dry kernels of grain in your hand? Wheat, rye, corn? Do you not discover a reverence welling up inside as you rub them between your fingers . . . as the truth dawns that the very mystery of life itself exists within those tiny grains? *Inside,* in the germ. Where the physical eye cannot see.

Where is the life of an egg?

In the yolk.

What do all three have in common—the egg, the kernel, and the rose?

They all contain life. *Hidden* life!

Life that is invisible except to those eyes that search for it—and therein lies the mystery!

9

THE GREATEST
HIDDEN MYSTERY
OF ALL

A while ago we took our first steps up into the
hills toward his presence, into the upper reaches
where we have not been before. Now pause.
Look around you. Imagine your Father
accompanying you.

Are you a little more used to him now? Is a
familiarity beginning to set in? Has friendship
begun?

As we move along, imagine your Father smiling
beside you. It is he who has beckoned you, not me.

"I have something to show you," he says. "A
small truth, but a worthwhile one. If you can
understand it, it will be the first of many such
truths I will show you."

You glance up and return his smile. "Oh yes, Father! I am eager for whatever you have to show me. Please reveal truth to me. Especially show me how to call you Father, and more of what your Fatherhood means."

"Do you find the upward course pleasant, now that the mists are thinning?"

"Yes."

"Then let us look more to what this high country has to tell us. Kneel down," says the Father, releasing the hand by which he has been leading you upward into his world, into the air and garden of his creation. "Scoop up a handful of the earth around one of these roses."

"Look at what you've picked up," he says. "Is there anything special about it?"

"It is only soil," you say.

"Do you see color there? Do you smell the perfume of the rose?"

"Certainly not."

But in truth, in God's idea of what makes a

rose a rose, all those qualities are there in your hand.

Perhaps the glory of the rose is indeed embodied in the flower you lift to your nostrils. But the life—the mystery—is contained in the handful of dirt you scooped up from below!

Once you clip a stalk from the plant, immediately the blossom begins to die. As long as its roots extend deep into the earth, the plant lives and thrives and continues to bear a wonderful profusion of color. But take it out of the soil, and instantly the life is gone.

What do you see in that soil in your hand?

Nothing but dirt, wouldn't you say? Place it on a woman's dress, or upon the floor of your living room, or on a plate at your dinner table, and everyone would stare aghast.

Dirt is something we purge from our home and our clothes, and before we eat the vegetables of our gardens, we carefully wash off all traces of residue from the ground.

Curious, is it not, that this low, despised commodity we call dirt should be the very transmitter of life itself to everything that grows on the face of God's earth?

God hides life in the most out-of-the-way places, even in those things that are looked upon with contempt.

Pause again. Glance up into the treetops around you and then to the sky beyond.

Can you not sense the beginning of a change already? Do you not feel more in touch with the high-reaching instinct of your nature?

Breathe in deeply again. Does it not seem good to know that the Father is nearby, that you can come and go in his presence without anxiety and fear, and that he has many pleasant secrets to reveal to you?

Most of all, does it not seem wonderful to realize that there is a smile on his face and that he welcomes you into his presence?

Five minutes with the Father. Every moment

spent thus with him, listening to him,
conversing with him, deepens the knowing and
adds meaning when we look up and call him
Father.

Again it is time for the reminder: Be not in a hurry in your quest. It will take time to develop the intimacy you prayerfully seek.

Close your eyes. Descend inwardly to your quiet closet of communion, and there whisper again: "Reveal truth to me. Show me how to call you Father. Draw me into your presence."

All living things have much to tell us of their Maker. Mysteries . . . truths hidden from all but the most diligent and seeking of eyes.

Why is it so?

One would think God would desire that everyone know all they can about him. To our reasoning, it would seem his object would be to make all truth, and especially that which concerns his being and character, clear and plain and visible.

Why, then, are there so many mysteries?

Why are so many things hard to understand? Why is truth, of all life's commodities, the most difficult to come by? Why are the deepest things about God among the most obscure?

For the same reason that many of a garden's most spectacular wonders are hidden under the ground for all but a short season of the year, and even then are most thoroughly revealed only to those who love them.

Among the most significant of the words Jesus spoke, and among those most vital to be heeded and obeyed, are those he repeated often: "He who has ears to hear, let him hear."

To feel the full weight of this powerful command with which Jesus punctuated his important words, one must realize that he was not merely talking to Pharisees and hypocrites. He was also speaking to his followers.

Jesus knew well the divining truth that divides all the universe—that it is possible to see, and yet *not* see.

When speaking of our need to discover truths God has hidden away, we cannot limit our discussion to matters of belief and nonbelief. For Christians too— perhaps, even, above all—are required to discover deep truths *within* the walk of faith . . . truths that often aren't part of their daily life because the capacity to see with inner eyesight has not been developed as an intrinsic aspect of spiritual growth.

It is a matter of learning to *see* . . . with the right

eyes. And in a very real sense, it represents the beginning of spiritual maturity.

God's ways are often curious and full of mystery. Why is it that he always seems to *hide* himself, enclosing life and truth within mysterious outer shells that seem different than what they contain? No easily discerned answer presents itself to our intellect.

Yet whether or not we know *why* he chose it, this *is* one of God's methods. Somehow, though, another principle can be recognized here: that throughout every aspect of his work, God reveals truth only to those who truly seek it.

What a paradox we are given in Romans 1:19-20: Man can know all about God's nature by the things he has made, yet the Lord says truth has been obscured so that men will see and *not* understand. Also, the greater the truth, the more obscure he makes it, so that the finding of it must be all the greater a quest.

A huge screening process operates in constant interplay with world events and circumstances and teachings and words and situations and relationships—a process screening out truth seekers from self-seekers, just as farmers separate the wheat from the chaff at harvesttime.

Truth seekers discover layer upon layer of truth as they progress through life, whereas *self-seekers* become increasingly blinded to truth by the thickening screen of their self-preoccupation.

Therefore, God encloses the deepest truths in husks, so that truth seekers, those rare individuals who hungrily want to discover and know his ways, whatever the cost, will dig and search and pray and seek and ask . . . until light dawns in their hearts.

God chose to "hide his face" from the eyes of man and to reveal his being and character through the things he has made. He sent the Savior of men, the one who would be King over all the earth, the very King of kings, in a form none would recognize—a baby born of common folk.

George MacDonald wrote:

They all were looking for a king
To slay their foes, and lift them high:
Thou cam'st a little baby thing
That made a woman cry.

Why this is the process, who can know? But it *is* the process, inverted as it may be from human equations of reason and sense.

To *see* as Jesus commanded requires looking past the husks and shells, deep into the heart of all things. It requires spending more and more time in our own

quiet centers where true vision is developed and culti-
vated.

If it is true that God surrounds the largest of his
truths in the thickest of husks, we would expect the
greatest of his secrets to be among the most difficult to
find. The deepest and most hidden secret—the most
profound—is his *Fatherhood.* It is the most profound
because it lies at the core of God's nature itself.

God has allowed the Sonship of his nature to be
seeable to the eyes of man through Jesus. But God's
Fatherhood is hidden from earthbound eyes. It must
be penetrated in an altogether different manner.

The greatest truth to be found, therefore, is the
answer to this question: *Who is God the Father, and
what is he like?*

> *O God, help us understand. Reveal your truth to
> us, we ask you with all earnestness and humility.*
>
> *O our Father, increase our hunger to know you
> and to discover your ways! Give us minds and
> hearts and hands courageous and stout enough to
> dig, even unto weariness! Let us faint not. Bring
> your dawn to our heart!*

PART III
ABBA, FATHER!

---

*The First Plateau
of Our Journey*

10

GOD'S FATHERHOOD

The higher we walk, the more the fogs
dissipate behind us, and the clearer our vision
becomes.

Come, intrepid souls! Let us dare to probe
the reaches of God's being, to peel away the
husks, break open the shells, dig deeper into the
rich soils hidden from view . . . and, climbing
ever higher, find life with the Father and the
truths he has hidden there for us to find!

Ah, my dear friends! This is the essence of
walking up this path toward the high
places—holding his hand, listening to his voice
in the still, small, quiet regions of our heart,
watching where he is pointing, seeking the

clues, learning to spot them, discovering how to
see into and behind everything, probing the
mysteries and hidden meanings of life and the
universe—to discover the Father's being and
presence in and through it all!

He is holding our hand . . . and revealing
himself to us!

It is marvelous—like no other life imaginable.

With each step we take, we uncover more and
more of the hidden mysteries of the kingdom of
God, of which the deepest and most profound
is: What is the Fatherhood of God like?

———————

No doubt some of you, by this time, are growing
impatient with all the talk of mysteries and hidden
truths and are saying to yourselves, "Get on with it . . .
tell us about Fatherhood!"

I'm sorry, but I cannot *tell* you about Fatherhood.
I can only help you discover it for yourself. And the
first important part of that process is training yourself
to *see* in new ways. This is where it all begins, and it is
a slow, quiet learning process that cannot be hastened.

Why have we been talking about eggs and trees and roses and wheat? Because we have to train our eyes to *apprehend* Fatherhood in unexpected places. Nothing I can say to you later will be of the least benefit without these apprehending eyes.

Fatherhood exists . . . all about us. We have to learn to *see* it. First in grains of wheat and in the bud of the rose.

When those lessons are learned, the Spirit will take us to higher and higher plateaus, until at last we are capable of dwelling among the very mountain peaks themselves. To get there, however, we must learn to *discern* the Father's fingerprints in the world about us.

This is the first step in *knowing*. When we see his fingerprint, then we can begin to discover what kind of Father caused that fingerprint. Thus, slowly by degrees, his character begins to dawn in our heart.

———

The most important truth in all the universe can be stated in four words: *God is our Father.*

This is the central truth in all of life. The universe literally hangs together by it. Without this divine Fatherhood, there is no life, there is no love . . . there is no universe.

The degree to which we apprehend God's Fatherhood will be the degree to which we know life and the degree to which our life will be integrated, whole, and complete in relationship to the Creator who made us and to the surroundings in which he has placed us.

Seeking and finding God's Fatherhood is *the* great story, the essence of history, the very meaning and hidden mysterious thread weaving its way through every human life and every age. It is the story of God's people in the Bible. It is the reason Jesus came. It is the very essence of Jesus' two mighty prayers on the night before his death—with his disciples, and later in the garden as they slept.

In this pilgrimage we have undertaken, we are following in the footsteps of Jesus, our elder Brother, who throughout his life had to seek God and pray for increasing depths to be revealed to him concerning the divine Fatherhood, for he himself was occasionally in doubt about his Father's will.

Imagine it—even Jesus himself had to seek this "knowing" of his Father's character and being, in just the same way we do! He had to "get to know" the Father too.

Indeed, he is our Brother . . . our example and our trailblazer in this quest!

When we read the Gospels with our newly trained eyes, we begin to see that God's Fatherhood is the single truth toward which Jesus *always* points. It was the focal point of his mission on earth.

In this mission, however, Jesus forged new ground. Aside from a few instances, throughout the Old Testament God had not been perceived as a Father at all. There was no doctrine of the Trinity—no concept of Father, no knowledge of Son, no awareness of Holy Spirit. God was Yahweh, God was "one." *Father* was arguably the last term anyone would have used to describe God.

The Jews in Jesus' day viewed God primarily as a Judge, nor was their religion a personal one. Moses and David had walked in intimate friendship with God, but not so the masses. The Law was to be obeyed, and the Almighty Judge called Yahweh stood ready to render judgment when it was broken.

Greek and Roman secularists and philosophers, on the other hand, viewed "God" or "the gods" as either an abstract principle or pure myth.

Nowhere in the theological or philosophical world of Jesus' time, then, was divine character equated with Fatherhood.

Jesus did not merely "make all things new" by bringing the new life of the second birth, as he explained to Nicodemus. He made new as well the prevailing perception of who God was. He broke apart the "oneness" of God's being into its three constituent parts.

He declared: "I am the *Son*. I will make life possible by my example, my teaching, and by giving my life for you. When I go from you, I will send the *Spirit* to reveal truth to you and to give you power to live the new life."

And throughout his life, over and over Jesus emphasized: "Come to my *Father*, pray to my *Father*, know my *Father*, seek my *Father*. I will show you the way to him . . . but *he* is the source of the life itself."

Fatherhood was the reason Jesus could work miracles, the reason he was born into a family, the reason he died, the reason he rose. The Atonement and the Resurrection were the Father's doing, wrought and made possible through Jesus' obedience. Jesus had nothing else in all the world to do—and he said so—but to point us to the Father.

"If you have seen me," he said, "you have seen the Father."

Thus, the question arises: Have we truly seen either Jesus *or* the Father? Seen them as he meant us to see them?

That is why we must train our eyes to *see*, first in the small things, that we might later behold the larger.

It behooves us to look with more dedication and

diligence into the Gospels to discover the true nature of both Father and Son. For learning to live as the Father's children is the only means whereby the world will come to know the Father Jesus came to reveal.

11

ABBA, FATHER

It has been the custom among valley dwellers to assume that anything having to do with spiritual things automatically makes use of inner or "spiritual" eyes.

Not so, my friends.

Here is a truth that it takes mature humility to see: Realities of spiritual truth can be seen with either the eyes of the flesh—physical eyes that ascertain merely what is evident and visible on the surface—or the eyes of the spirit—that deep, inner sight.

It is possible to scrutinize every New Testament doctrine imaginable and to fill in with a certain accuracy an intellectually consistent informational grid about God and his work . . . yet all the while to see but an incomplete, sketchy, and highly abridged version of spiritual reality. When spiritual truth is viewed with the wrong set of eyes, the eyes of the flesh, it is seen through a glass darkly.

When human intellect leads the way, building precept upon precept from earlier doctrines put forth by human intellects equally looking only on the surface of scriptural truth, a curtailed theology satisfying to the equations set by human reason is all that can possibly result.

He who has ears to hear, let him hear.

The reality of God's Fatherhood is to be discovered in that region of reality where the two kinds of seeing cannot be intermingled. Its equations are not equal by human spiritual reason. Those who would follow the Master toward the high places of relationship with his Father must learn to explore the mysteries and deep truths hidden from those whose eyes are limited to the intellectual world, seeing by the rules of earthbound spiritual mathematics.

Between the clearly discernible regions of truth and falsehood lies a gray shadowy land of partial truth, whose inhabitants live according to spiritual principles but apprehend them with fleshly eyes. As we make our way toward the high places, we will encounter many such individuals, attempting to live mountain truths in low-lying, hollowed-out ravines among the hills where the valley fogs still infiltrate, blocking out the sun just as severely as in the valley we have left behind.

Pray for them as we pass, dear friends, for how desperately they need to look up and behold the mountains!

————————

Everything changed when Jesus came.

Salvation became personal. Living as God's sons and daughters became personal. God's being became personal.

The triune personality of the Godhead is clearly
evident from the opening chapters of Genesis, but God
did not make the constituent parts of his nature discernible and available to man until the fullness of time
when Jesus came to earth.

At that point he peeled away the shell, the husk. He
tore down the veil that had hidden his presence. He
opened up the "oneness" of Yahweh that had been the
core of Judaism throughout the Old Testament and
said to man, "Here are the three parts of me, which you
may now personally and individually and intimately
relate yourselves to."

For the first time he allowed man to peer inside,
into the very depths of his being. Not just peer inside
. . . *he invited man to come live with him there!*

What was it men and women found when they
looked beyond the veil, when they gazed into the
depths of God's being?

They discovered the Son, Jesus himself! A sinless
Man, a loving Friend, an understanding Brother who
was willing to die for them, that they might not perish
from sin.

When he went away, they further discovered a
consoling, guiding, truth-loving Spirit, the very Spirit
of God whom Jesus had promised he would send to
remain with them forever.

But what else did they discover?

Just what Jesus had told them they would find—a loving, tender, forgiving, patient, warm, generous Father who wants only the best for his children and who will spare nothing to lavish his love upon them, thus bringing them to the pinnacle of their personhood, the very mountaintop of existence. It is a picture of God's being and purpose in human life far different from what those of Jesus' day imagined.

The writer of Hebrews opens his letter with the magnificent words that illuminate this huge shift in divine revelation: "In the past God spoke to our forefathers through the prophets at many times and in various ways, but in these last days he has spoken to us by his Son."

The Sonship of Jesus necessitated a divine Fatherhood, a way of seeing God that was utterly foreign to the prevailing religious mentality of Jesus' day. Alas, all these centuries later, we still have not apprehended what the Son was trying to tell us about the Father he loved so dearly!

Of all the changes brought by Jesus in what constituted a "spiritual life," intimacy with God as Father was the most astonishing and revolutionary.

Jesus rose before daybreak and went out into the hills to be alone with God. Who was it he sought there?

The Incomprehensible Almighty Sovereign King of the Universe? That Great and Dreadful Holy Presence upon whose face no man could look and live? The Omnipotent Lawgiver of Old Testament Judaism? The Holy One who could not abide sin in his Presence? The Just Judge of the Universe who would decide the ultimate eternal fate of every creature?

No.

Jesus rose before daybreak to be alone with his Father, to speak intimately with him, calling him *Abba*.

Abba was the term a child used when he addressed his father. It was probably the word Jesus used when talking to Joseph . . . Abba . . . father . . . *daddy*. It conveyed warmth and family respect, but in regard to God it was an unheard of familiarity.

Within Judaism there is no indication it had ever been a form of address toward God. Jesus was the first so to employ the word.

If Jesus was truly God's Son, then it is understandable that he would make use of this form of intimate address. But the thunderous truth is this: *He told all men to follow his example.*

The Lord's Prayer began with *Abba*, as Jesus told his disciples how to speak to God. He gave them the right to use this term of intimacy and familiarity—the intimacy of divine *Daddy*ness with Almighty God, the Creator of the heavens and earth!

In that moment, the entire foundation of our relationship with God was changed: Jesus declared that God was forevermore to be our *daddy!*

You may approach the Father closely and intimately now, he said—yourselves!

The God of fire and thunder, the God upon whom no man can look, the Holy and Almighty, the Sovereign of Sinai, the great and terrible has now also become your *Daddy . . . Abba.*

He loves you and will now forgive you your sin. You have only to go to him!

The veil that hid the Holy of Holies was rent in two. We are invited into his presence, there to dwell with him in continual intimacy.

12

IMAGINING THE WORLD'S MOST LOVING DADDY

Imagine yourself for a moment, as we walk along, as an orphan.

Jesus will soon be joining us to take us the rest of the way up the mountain. Let us imagine what he might say when we meet him.

"Come, my friend. I want you to meet my daddy. He is the most wonderful Father there ever has been. I have told him of our friendship, and he wants to adopt you as his very own child. He desires that you become part of our family!"

What could possibly be more wonderful—to have a father who wants you to be his very own child, to be part of his family! Never had you dreamed such good fortune would come to you!

Eagerly you take the hand of Jesus and follow.
On the way you daydream about what this
"most wonderful Father" might be like.

Jesus called him wonderful, so that must
mean he is full of love. How could he be
anything but kind and generous and patient,
attentive and interested in your thoughts,
forgiving of your mistakes and shortcomings?

If he is anything like Jesus, he must be all
those things. Jesus said he was very much like
his Father, and you have known Jesus long
enough to know what a kind and loving friend
he has been.

Surely this wonderful Father must take care
of his children, protecting them from harm,
providing for their needs, comforting them in
distress.

He must be warm and tender and
compassionate, the kind of Father upon whose
lap no child would hesitate to climb, there to
snuggle against his bosom within the wrap of

his large and kindhearted arms. He must be a
smiling Father who lavishes his young one with
kisses and hugs as he whispers, "I love you, my
child. You are dear and precious to me. I will
keep my arms snugly around you forever and
will hold you as long as you will let me. You
may get down, but I will never set you down off
my lap nor send you away. It is my delight to
love you and to know that you love me."

He might be stern, you think to yourself.
Surely a perfect Father would not put up with
misbehavior, and might even have to discipline
you from time to time. But, you conjecture
further, you would not mind that so much, for
you would know he was doing it only because
he loved you and wanted the best for you.

———————

It may strike some readers as unfortunate that the term
father occupies such a pivotal role in God's nature, for
in many minds today that term conjures up images
contradictory to these pleasant daydreams.

Today's father is the butt of every sitcom joke and has a hard time getting his own kids to turn off the TV. He is either a watered-down nonentity or the scapegoat for his children's later problems and personality hangups.

In the ancient patriarchal societies to which Jesus spoke, however, the father was a vital and important figure. A Roman father had power of life or death over his children. A good father could be extraordinarily good, a bad father could be extraordinarily bad.

Western culture is no longer patriarchal. Therefore, when we say "father," we are not thinking of the same image Jesus was.

Father, however, was the term Jesus used. His Father was his *Father*, not his mother.

To escape the asphyxiating fogs of valley misperceptions, our thinking must widen—not to throw away the earthly forms of the word, but rather to cast aside the shackles and constraints they impose upon our capacity to see God as he truly is.

How much larger might true and perfect Fatherhood be?

As we thus widen our image of Fatherhood beyond its earthly constraints, a startling truth results: The masculine *and* feminine forms of earthly in-God's-image–ness become drawn up into the unifying whole.

Human motherhood and fatherhood *both* combine to make up this divine picture.

It is regrettable that emotionally heated connotations must accompany our use of masculine and feminine terms, for their subtle notions of modernity throw up stumbling blocks along our way.

Women who took offense earlier at the masculinity said to be inherent in God's Fatherhood may now find themselves joined by men taking offense at femininity entering the divine personality.

Make no mistake. This joint masculinity and femininity cannot be envisioned according to any earthly images. Within the Godhead they are taken to higher levels, glorified, fulfilled, given their perfect expression as God intended all creation to reflect distinctive aspects of his nature.

We are being given a place to live within the divine "familyness" of the very Godhead itself!

Why do we begin thus, with the imagination? Are we not bound to come to know God the Father on the basis of what Scripture tells us?

Certainly.

The imagination is merely a doorway.

God has placed the instinct toward Fatherhood deep within every human breast. Everything in us, by nature, points toward our Father, including the imag-

ination. When one attempts to imagine God, therefore, free from any preconceptions to the contrary, the
compass of God-created instinct within cannot help
but point in a generally true direction.

These are not fruitless and vain imaginings, but
rather the God-implanted instinct after true Fatherhood expressing itself through the imagination he created for this very purpose.

The imagination wants to bring good and kind and
loving images to mind because God put those visions
of himself within us so that we would know what his
Fatherhood is like.

13
THE HUSK

Did you find it difficult to imagine the world's most loving Daddy?

One who cannot imagine the Father and conceive of what he is like will have difficulty scaling the peaks still ahead. An unimaginative outlook makes of faith a monotonous affair, enfeebling the capacity to walk fully with him.

Why is it so difficult to imagine pure and unreserved goodness at the intrinsic core of Fatherhood?

Because the husks are so thick surrounding the earthly images with which we are familiar. Unfortunately these husks have, till now, comprised our only clear pictures of what Fatherhood might be like.

The imagination is not an area within the human disposition that we have allowed to further spiritual growth. In fact, it is customary to consider it as emerging out of man's fallen nature.

Not so. Imagination, like everything God created, is good.

Henceforth, we will make more and more use of it as a God-given tool, a walking stick to help us in our climb, stretching our capacity to dwell in Fatherhood with him.

———————

As we have already seen and discussed, every atom of the universe reflects something about its Creator's being and personality and nature. The divine fingerprint exists everywhere.

In the very act of creation, God left his mark. In all he has ever touched, the divine fingerprint remains. No erasing agent exists with the capacity to rub out his identifying signature. To know God requires learning to behold those invisible fingerprint lines. We must then use our new ways of seeing and our imagination to identify his signature and to apprehend his Fatherhood in those fingerprints.

Why did God institute earthly fatherhood?

Was it only so men and women could bring forth sons and daughters to keep the human race alive? As we inquired earlier of God, is the reason earthly fathers exist chiefly one of begetting . . . or is there a greater purpose?

Yes, certainly . . . but what?

He created earthly fathers primarily to offer a picture of what *he* is like.

Fathers, however, don't do a very good job of showing us God's nature.

The mystery deepens.

God created roses, and they perfectly fulfill their calling. God created the sun, the sky, and the heavens to reflect his glory, and they too fulfill their callings. God created the animal kingdom, and every animal, large and small, fulfills its inborn calling.

God created earthly fatherhood to reflect his nature more than all these others . . . yet earthly fathers do *not* fulfill this most holy calling.

The physical husk surrounding the spiritual truth is indeed a thick one. How are we to penetrate it?

Why did God select the imperfect to reflect the perfect?

Ah, God our Father, do we doubt your wisdom? Give us eyes to see that we might behold your purposes in the midst of our earthbound reasonings. Open our eyes wide, Father, to the worlds of Fatherhood you would establish within us!

Remember, the greater the truth, the more obscure God makes it, so that the finding of it must occasion all the greater a quest.

The process of discovering God's Fatherhood is multidirectional and multidimensional. It isn't a matter of writing down attributes and adopting prescriptions that say, "God is such-and-such," and then saying to oneself, "Ah, now I grasp God's Fatherhood."

God's Fatherhood, the *one* truth he wants all men and women to discover, is—because it is the *largest* truth—one of the most obscured to worldly vision with one of the thickest husks.

In fatherhood itself, even though we don't readily see it, God has left the divine impression of his being. Within the very *fact of fatherhood,* earthly husks and all, are stored away vast worlds of truth about God's Fatherhood, having little or no connection with the godliness or cruelty by which a given man expresses it.

Because Fatherhood is the central life, the central

love, the central energy, the central meaning of the universe, and the most important truth for his creatures to grasp if they are to know life, God established the universe to function in such a way that a smaller kind of fatherhood, a picture of his own, would reside at the center of human life. He thus ordained "fathers" and "mothers" as the procreators of earthly existence, passing on life and love to their offspring. He then went to enormous lengths to explain to parents how they were to function in this role and accomplish the task he had set before them.

The whole process of earthly fatherhood and motherhood and childhood was to combine in such a way as to create a magnificent threefold portrait of the Godhead, of our heavenly Maker and Creator, and of the Fatherhood that gives life to everything in the universe.

As in all things, sin interrupted and corrupted the process. The enemy has gone to great lengths to infiltrate the family unit, to discredit the earthly symbol of God's establishing. Instead of pointing us *to* God our Father, the incompleteness of earthly fatherhood has, with Satan's help, embittered sons and daughters *against* their parents and, in doing so, blinded them to the magnificence of God's Fatherhood.

Thus has been dulled, almost beyond recognition, the essential human instinct—that created yearning to look up and behold our Father. A gigantic stone sits in the middle of the road preventing each one of us from even thinking clearly on the subject, let alone getting past the obstacle.

For my own sons, it is I, their earthly father.

For me, it's my father.

You have your own stone in the person of your own father.

I tell my own sons: I am a woefully imperfect vessel for carrying such a lofty and marvelous truth—that God loves them utterly and completely and is doing everything in his creative power to reveal that love in mutual relationship with them.

As much as I love my sons, however, I don't love them *utterly.* I'm a flawed, selfish, incomplete, imperfect human being. Compared with God's love, mine is a meager demonstration indeed. I am subject to the full range of human tendencies that obstruct love from being fully felt, fully expressed, and fully lived out between men and women, parents and children, brothers and sisters, friends and acquaintances.

We were put on this earth to love, but none of us knows how to do it very well. The earthly image of fatherhood, designed to show us how, is flawed. It is an imperfect vessel.

If earthly fathers are intended to be mirrors, reflecting back some image of God, there is no denying they are cracked and broken. The image they reflect is incomplete or distorted.

There are millions of broken mirrors in the world, including the one each of us was born gazing into. Yet we still have to find our true Father.

The trouble is, many people, seeing that the mirror is broken or shattered, and embittered by whatever their own experience has been, turn their backs and walk away, never to discover God's Fatherhood at all.

In fact it was never the role of earthly fathers and mothers to offer other than partial images. They yield but a portrayal of God's Fatherhood, in the same way that a tree or the sky or the seasons or a fragrant rose produce true but partial pictures of certain aspects of God's nature.

The common fallacy is to equate the fatherhood of one's earthly father with an accurate representation of God's heavenly Fatherhood. Though not intentionally, or even consciously, we draw this equal sign in our mistaken equation at a deep subconscious level very, very early in life.

However, as life progresses and we grow and mature and learn, we fail to mature in this most vital area—we fail to learn the skills of higher spiritual mathematics necessary to enable us to undo that false human computation. The fatherhood equation must be rewritten. Yet it takes high-mountain vision to figure out the algebra of the divine formula.

Earthly fatherhood is intended only as a temporary enclosure for something far, far greater that it was God's intent for all to seek and ultimately discover— the perfection of Fatherhood we find in him!

Once we allow the lives of our earthly fathers to carry out the work for which they were intended (imperfect and incomplete, yet pointing upward, causing us to ask, Where is perfect and complete Fatherhood?), then (and only then) are we ready to scale the heights toward the uppermost regions of the Fatherhood of our heavenly Father.

> *O God, reveal truth to us at this moment! Let us put away the smallness of our responses. Holy Spirit, we ask you to blow away the clouds that obscure our vision with cramped images of past hurts and disappointments. Show us the divine interrelation between fatherhood and Fatherhood. Teach us what* **father** *means as well as* **Father***. Help us progress along these high pathways of our journey, ever deeper into the mountains toward your presence. Give us eyes to see truth.*
>
> *O God, the cry of our heart is that we might learn to call you Father!*

14
FATHERHOOD REQUIRES CHILDNESS

The gray valley fog is cancerously lethal, yet it brings a certain comfort to the lungs. A sting accompanies our first gulps of the pure air above it, not altogether pleasant, like a sharp and frightful jolt of electric current through our system.

Not yet used to the invigoration of life that will follow, we gasp at first inhalation, shocked, trying to recatch our breath, wondering if it is life or death this mountain air brings.

It stings because there is a cost to ourselves, an unpleasantness that will continue as long as we insist on being our own master. There is a price to be paid before we can call him *Abba*.

But the sting of the air above the suffocating cloud is merely temporary. Indeed, we will soon learn to thrive on that goading, provoking keenness, realizing that we have never felt such vital life as this bracing air jolts into us.

The fog may be comfortable and easier to breathe, but it is sure to deaden the higher sensitivities of both heart and brain. The pure air may sting, but its chemical formula is what our lungs were made to breathe. Though it seems we at first choke with painful gasps that will kill us, this is the only air that will not result in our death.

What does it mean, that we may come to God with personal and familial address, that we can look upward, seeking his face, and call him by that most private and confidential word, *Father*—and even the more intimate *Abba!*—as if there were only the two of us in all the universe? Of what is this intimacy with God comprised?

What prevents even diligent seekers from apprehending this most central theme of the gospel story, causing them to satisfy their spiritual hungers with lesser meat? What so obscures even God's spiritual offspring from perceiving with clarity that which was the guiding truth of Jesus' every moment?

If the instinct exists within the men and women of God's making to look *up* to Fatherhood, why do they, like the animals, seek horizontal fulfillment only? Why do they turn their eyes away from that very thing for which their spirit yearns at the deepest levels?

The answer to this pivotal question can be stated with far more simplicity than its truth can be translated into life. It is this: There can be no fatherhood without corresponding *childness.*

To acknowledge God as Father requires that I acknowledge myself as his child. Acknowledge that there is One above me, One who will *always* be above me—older than me, bigger than me, wiser than me . . . infinite where I am finite, eternal where I am temporal, Creator where I am merely created. In every way the brain can imagine, he is the More, I am the less. He is the Initiator; I can only respond. I am utterly, unconditionally, and in all ways his child.

My reliance upon him is total. I cannot live, cannot love, cannot think, cannot feel, cannot reason, cannot choose, cannot create apart from his spirit breathing life through me. It is a relationship of dependence that I will never outgrow.

The very notion of self-rule is dead altogether.

The *Godness, authority,* and supreme *masculinity* of Fatherhood merge into a finality of overlordship from which there is not even the possibility of escape . . . ever. Ultimate Fatherhood is eternally over us.

Such are the components, the chemical formula, of the blue mountain air above the gray valley clouds. No wonder its first entry into our lungs stings! It goes against everything valley society has ingrained in us and everything we would prefer to believe.

The man or woman who resists this overarching truth by which the universe hangs together, holding out the vain and impossibly foolish fantasy that we may exist somehow out from under it, is destined to a life of constantly bumping against the painfully pricking goads of attempted self-reliance and self-rule.

When in the pure air above we identify God as Father, however, it is not a relationship of dependence begrudgingly acknowledged, but one joyfully *welcomed.* Then first does such a one understand the overlordship of the universe. Recognizing the masculinity, the authority, and the Godness of divine Fatherhood, we *choose* to walk in our childness in submission to the Father.

If the greatest stumbling block to recognizing the magnificence of God's Fatherhood is earthly fatherhood, then the greatest stumbling block to intimacy with the Father himself is the *independence* every human soul craves.

Independence: *I am my own . . . I need none other.*

Here is the great barrier to the fulfillment of our destiny, the world's single great evil, the cause of all unhappiness abroad in the land, the source of all our frustrations and anxieties and that nagging sense dogging our heels that life is somehow not all it ought to be.

Independence. It is the great lie of the universe. The original sin that turned Satan into the enemy of God's every purpose. It is the inbred orientation that is at utter odds with the one necessity of vertical significance—bowing before One greater.

Independence says: *I will be no one's child. Childness—Ha! I outgrew that years ago! I am an independent entity, sufficient unto myself. I will not submit. No one will tell me what to do. I am my own master. I will call no one Father.*

Without acknowledged childness, intimacy with Fatherhood is impossible.

Though childness is required, however, it is not something even the Father can *make* us do.

Such accedence, such submission, such laying

down of independence, such willing abandonment of one's life into the hands of Another is brought about by choice. Engaging the will into chosen harmony with our Maker brings the mind, heart, and soul into alignment behind it.

Thus, if we are kept from the very intimacy we long for, if we do not make closer approach to that Father-hood toward which our instinct draws us, if we do not drink of that water with which our soul thirsts to be satisfied, if we refuse to reach toward that high destiny that is the home in which our heart was made to dwell which represents the pinnacle of our personhood and being . . . we do so by our own choice.

Father, help us to see that you are not some cruel celestial taskmaster determined to pin us under your thumb. Help us to recognize this most deadly of all lies, masterminded by a society whose granaries of truth have gone bankrupt—that independence leads to happiness.

May we recognize the rightness, the truth, and the contentment inherent within a full interactive dependence upon and with the Father of Jesus Christ as we extend our quest into the uppermost regions whence spring the only wells of fulfillment and abundance to be found in all creation!

PART IV
A GOD TO
CALL FATHER

———

*Glimpses of the
Mountain Estate*

15

CREATION OF THE UNIVERSAL FAMILY

We are now high up, well away from the valley. The air is thin, crisp, and so fresh! And we can see so clearly. Vision and stamina, indeed all our physical senses, seem vastly improved.

Yet do you not find the way occasionally difficult—even those serious among you who have ventured this far out of the valley toward the mountaintops where Fatherhood intimacy dwells?

Having laid aside those earlier encumbrances, hungry to breathe the reviviscent mountain air despite its stings, thirsty to find the source of those gushing tonic-filled waters, and eagerly

now attempting to press toward the inner
reaches of God's being . . . what prevents you
from running and leaping with positive delight
in the Father's Fatherhood?

Why are the mountains still so difficult to
scale?

———————

What we are to apprehend from our first images of
Fatherhood is a simple enough, though foundational,
lesson. It is so simple, in fact, that it escapes most of
humankind. It is just this: Where there is an imperfect
reflection, there must be a perfect Source of the reflection. If there is an incomplete fatherhood, there must
be a perfect Fatherhood. Therefore, if I am to be a true
man or woman, I must seek to find that true Source,
that higher Fatherhood.

What prevents God's creatures from entering into
that happiest, that highest, that most wonderful and
holy relationship that he intended?

Society and modernity, yes, pressure against it.

The self-motivated will of man, yes, makes choices
contrary to it.

Sin, yes, infiltrates every corner of man's being with

the lie of independence, that most serious of all preventative inoculations to ward off intimacy.

But what prevents us—you and me—from laying hold of the very relationship that everything within us cries out for?

This question probes the very bedrock of our spiritual existence. To find the answer requires journeying back toward the distant foundations of all things. Back to the very beginning in Genesis 1—back to the sixth day of creation.

There we seek, not for abstract history, but for ourselves. For what purpose did God create man on that significant sixth day of creation?

Who among his fallen world of creatures can probe the infinitely ageless, creatively motivated heart of God? His infinitude is unknowable by our finiteness. To ask *why* God does anything is rendered contradictory by definition. He is not subject to the *why*s of reason.

God *is,* therefore . . . *everything!*

What he wills simply *is.* I AM is his name. No *why* even fits into that I-AM–ness.

He delights, however, when we apply ourselves more deeply to understand his ways, seeking not the contradictory *why*s of man's independence, but eager to enter into the *divine why*s of the Father's plan.

Thus let us dare suggest the following: that God created man to expand the family of his Fatherness.

The Son within the godhood was a holy expression of the divine Trinity. But the divine Son was an only child. And the creative heart of Love beat with creating love-energy toward more sons and daughters whom he could bring into his family as brothers and sisters to his Son.

"Let *us* make man in *our* image," God said. The divine family—us—already walked the earth prior to day six, but the Father of that divine family desired more creatures to partake in it.

They would be of a lesser nature, it is true, and far more vulnerable. But the divine Firstborn would be their elder Brother, and he would help them learn to live within the divine family, even sacrificing for them if need be. He would be all an elder Brother should be. And in spite of their lesserness and susceptibility to forces outside the family, they would still retain the image of their Creator-Father, for his fingerprint could never be eradicated from their hearts.

So the Father created man, and the family of his universe was made. And he blessed them, giving them dominion and wisdom and food and companionship and pleasure and the most wondrous place to live imaginable.

He created these younger brothers and sisters to fellowship with him and his firstborn Son, to walk with them in the Garden in the cool of the day, to work the earth of his creation, to reproduce, to tend the lower creatures of his unbounded divine imagination, to rule the earth, and to fully enjoy all the goodness he had made.

Everything God made was good. Including his children.

God saw that it was good.

God saw that it was good!

God saw that it was *good!!*

So vital and significant is this truth that God instructed the writer of the Genesis account to repeat it seven times—the number of perfection—punctuating it after the creation of man with the words *very good.*

That is the resounding truth of Genesis 1: "God created man in his own image. . . . God saw all that he had made, and it was very good. And there was evening, and there was morning—the sixth day."

Incredible as it seems, there is a certain branch of pietism that speaks of some of the old-fashioned scriptural virtues, such as goodness, as if they are actually bad things. This shortsightedness isolates a verse such as Isaiah 64:6—"All of us have become like one who is unclean, and all our righteous acts are like filthy rags"—and erects an entire theology around it, ignoring the sevenfold declaration of Genesis *from God's own mouth.* Misguided theologies result, putting black above white, making hell a deeper truth in the economy of eternity than God's victory, and declaring the starting point for the gospel to be sin instead of love.

Those who make sin the foundational starting point for attempting to understand the nature of man do God's creation a grievous wrong. With that sand-built base as their starting point, they are able to understand neither man nor the Father. Rather than undergirding their theologies with the eternal bedrock of Genesis 1—the beginning!—they begin their erroneous expositions at Genesis 3.

They come at truth from the wrong angle altogether, thus entirely missing the vital point that *goodness lies deeper in the heart of man's nature than the sin, which came later and entered from the outside.*

Goodness lies deeper in man because God put himself there. It was *very* good!

Goodness is intrinsic to man's nature; sin is not. Sin is the corrupting virus that has temporarily contaminated goodness. But even sin itself cannot alter the truth of Genesis 1:31 that echoes throughout all eternity.

Goodness lies deep in the bedrock of the universe, not merely because what God created was good, but because goodness is intrinsic to God's nature itself.

Do we seek to know what the Father is like? We have not far to look. We have only to open our Bibles and read one chapter—the very first chapter. *Good, good, good, good, good, good . . . very good!*

The divine fingerprint of what he created reflects who God is at every point! Perfect (sevenfold) goodness.

Following the mighty creation of Genesis 1 came the triumphant unveiling of God's ultimate and perfect blueprint of life within his newly created family—the majestic glory of Genesis 2. Here was *life* as God intended it—*good* life!

Genesis 2, in a sense, is a chapter detailing perfection. It opens with rest, with a holy day, because creation was fully accomplished . . . and fully good. It then goes on to describe in detail the kind of life God intended to enjoy with his creatures. A beautiful Garden was to be their home. Trees were planted that were pleasing to look at and pleasing to eat.

What provision! Not mere trees, but good and pleasing trees. Not just some trees . . . *all* kinds of trees!

Did Adam and Eve need to eat of the tree of the

knowledge of good and evil? Of course not. They had every other kind of tree imaginable, as well as every other generous provision.

It was an enormous Garden. Four mighty rivers flowed through it. The very word *Garden* may give us an entirely limited impression. For all we know, this Garden where God dwelt with man could have comprised the entire Middle East . . . or perhaps half the globe.

Life with God in the Garden was anything but dull. It was a life of constantly receiving good from the hands of God.

God gave and gave and gave . . . and everything he gave was very good!

He gave Adam a helper, Eve. He gave both of them all they needed. He gave them the privilege of working with him to tend the Garden.

He gave them food. He gave them freedom. He gave them pleasure. He gave them wisdom and knowledge. He gave them dominion over the earth. He gave them innocence.

Most of all, he gave them fellowship with himself, the God who had made them.

He gave them nothing less than a *perfect* life.

Perfection everywhere!

How long they lived in the Garden in this perfect

and innocent state it is impossible to conjecture, but it clearly went on for an extended period. Time enough for Adam to name *all* the birds and *all* the beasts of the ground.

Genesis 2 is one of the Bible's most significant chapters, offering limitless insight into the purposes of God's heart!

16

THE DEMON LIES
OF GENESIS 3

We are beginning to scale the mountains in earnest. Snow lies all about us now, sometimes in high drifts. Occasionally we glance upward, wondering how much higher we may go and still live. Yet an invigoration accompanies any potential danger.

Goodness is the air we must learn to breathe if we are to travel far in this region. As familiar as we are with the word, however, breathing its air—living by the vitality of its astounding and overarching truth—is an unfamiliar exercise.

Even though we are leaving the valley fogs behind, however, there are still dangers in these mountains—steep precipices and tricky chasms

and our fears of avalanche—that would keep us
from apprehending the true glory of Genesis 2
life.

After the creation of God's universal family, the enemy
corrupted its goodness with the evil virus called sin.

Two demons, following the pride of Satan's rebellion, were sent to tempt man's brain and then enter his
heart . . . and sunder him from his Creator.

The first we have already spoken of. He is still with
us, and his lies still perpetrate his dissevering work. His
evil name is *independence.* Though I call it his name, I
will not venerate his lying nature with the uppercase.

"Did God really say you could not eat?" his treacherous tongue whispers. "Nah, you mustn't bother
about that. You don't *need* God. You can live without
him."

The lie of independence.

The lie that broke and destroyed the innocent
childness of life in the Garden.

No more insidious and perfect demon could have
been sent to destroy the Genesis 2 relationship between the Father and his created children. How lethal
is the spirit of independence, absolutely preventing a

right and humble child's heart before Fatherhood. Indeed, where independence reigns, Fatherhood itself becomes impossible.

Fatherhood *requires* childness—requires looking up and outside ourselves for direction to life. Childness *requires* submission to One greater—submission given by willing, self-denying choice. Such was Adam and Eve's Garden life in Genesis 2.

Submission born of coercion is no submission at all. Independence still reigns inwardly, whatever outward constraints have been artificially levied.

True childness is entered into by the full and happy choice of the child himself.

I will not be my own, says such a one. I have no desire to be my own.

I WILL to belong to another.

I CHOOSE not to be master of my own fate and destiny.

I WANT never to be independent about anything again.

I MAKE myself a child for the rest of my days.

I DECIDE to ask my Father what he would have of me.

I DESIRE to say, to think, to do, to plan, to hope for nothing but what the Father would want me to say, think, do, plan, or hope.

I ACCEPT that the Father knows what is best for me in ways far beyond my own capacity to know what is best.

I LAY DOWN all claim to anything resembling independence, that my Father might be all to me. Henceforth, I am wholly and utterly, in all ways, his child.

Fatherhood and independence are mutually exclusive. Neither can exist in the presence of the other.

Because young children have no choice but to live under the authority of and, in a sense, in submission to their parents, it is easy to assume that they are "children" in the full and proper sense.

Not so.

They are offspring. They have been placed within families as children, occupying the role of children, in order to be trained in the most elemental lesson in all the universe—that lesson which all men and women must one day learn: that they might desire to become *true children* indeed.

Alas, how very few learn to apprehend this foundational necessity for happiness and fulfillment!

In truth, the spirit of independence reigns more thoroughly within the heart of what we call a human child than in any other place within the created kingdom of planet earth. It is this independence that the

God-ordained and heaven-established family order was intended to purge out of him, that he might desire to put independence behind him and enter into a life with true *Fatherhood,* of which the earthly motherhood and fatherhood of his parents are but a faint and broken echo.

There is a childness into which we must all learn to grow, as well as a childhood we must all leave behind.

The latter we cannot help. There is no other way to come into being than as offspring of human parents. This process we share with the animal kingdom. But that unique calling of the divine within us, that instinct to cast our gaze upward, such is the stamp of God himself upon our nature. It is the call to become *his children!*

That is a childness that can only be entered into by the willing, submitted, self-denying choice to lay the independence of earthly childhood forever aside.

It is a childness of maturity. It represents the apex of human maturity, the very pinnacle of the human growth process.

To this choice, to this *growth into childness,* the earthly family—with its fatherhood, its motherhood, and its childhood—has forever been intended to lead. That it does help so few children to grow into childness is sad indication that few of its fathers and mothers are children of divine childness themselves.

Independence blocks the path of childness. It was the first lie told to man, and it has been preventing Fatherhood ever since.

————————

The instant the lie of the demon of independence was swallowed with the first disobedient action of man— the bite from the fruit of the tree—the second demon immediately entered the scene.

His evil name is *fear,* and his lie is equally insidious—and even more subtle.

"Have you sinned?" fear says. "Then God is going to punish you. Hide from him! It is your only chance."

Ah, the subtlety of his lying tongue! Replete, as are all lies from the enemy, with enough half-truth to masquerade as truth.

Even more easily than they believed the first lie, Adam and Eve now swallowed the second. Instantly they ceased to be the wise children of innocent childlikeness and became instead immature children of *childishness.*

They tried, foolish in their childish *independence,* to cover their nakedness. Then they attempted to hide from God himself, cowering in this newfound sensation called *fear.*

Foolish children!

Did you truly sin? Then perhaps your Father will have to punish you. But he is still your Father, and greater is his love than his disappointment that you have not obeyed him.

There is but one course open to you.

Run *to* him, not away from him!

Do not hesitate. *He is your refuge* against these lying demons.

Seek his help. Throw yourselves into the embrace of your Father! Tearfully confess your foolishness. Step back again into the childness in which you were created to live.

Become again his children.

That is your only chance.

Fear changes only two words from the full and glorious truth of our salvation! *Run to* him becomes *hide from* him . . . lie of lies!

What might the loving Father have done had Adam gone straight to him with confession and repentance, learning his lesson from believing the first demon's lie sufficiently to enable him to reject that from the second?

Discipline from the Father's hand would still have

been rendered; perhaps the gate to the Garden still would have been closed. But oh, how different thereafter might have been the fellowship between the Father and his family!

What restoration might have been in the Father's heart had the first Adam offered to make himself also the second, saying to his Maker, "Father, I have sinned. I have disobeyed your command. I was foolish to do so. I am sorry. The woman is blameless, for you gave me to rule over her. I take account for all. Take my life, for I deserve nothing less, and spare her. Let the whole of your curse fall upon me. Be it unto me according to your will."

But none of this was to be.

The demon called fear had gained a foothold from which it would never retreat. And the lie—that our Father is to be feared—persists today, still poisoning our capacity to correctly discern God's Fatherhood, preventing us from looking into his face, barring the way to intimacy.

The glory of Genesis 2 was undone.

17

ALL THE WAY BACK
TO THE GARDEN

Do you begin to sense voices calling you to come back to the valley?

The snows lay all around us now, thick and cold—surely we will not be able to keep climbing for long!

Has the high mountain air suddenly grown so thin of oxygen that your lungs feel even more pained and cramped?

Might you even hear independence itself saying, "There is nothing to breathe up here . . . you will die if you remain too long. This air is not good for you! Your self will have no room here to live as it is used to. Be careful. They are

trying to change you. They are trying to rob
you of your essential personality."

Many will be the voices of caution and
prudence attempting suddenly to exert
themselves, telling you that all this talk of
putting your independence to death is too
much, it is the final straw—you mustn't put up
with this!

Don't listen, my friends.

It is the same lie that spoke to Adam and Eve,
devising its subtleties especially for you,
attempting to break the Garden fellowship
between you and the Father and Son.

Press on with me!

The air of pure life, not death, lies ahead.

Death to independence . . . life to the spirit.

————————

Is harsh disciplinary Fatherhood anywhere near the
source of Creation?

Do we see it in Genesis 1? Is it to be found in the
interactive life within the Garden of Genesis 2, where

the Creator and his family enjoyed fellowship and walked together in intimacy—ruling, procreating, growing, and working together—according to the Father's purpose?

No. It came later, by necessity.

But not until Genesis 3—not until God's purposes and plan had been laid out and established for all to know and see.

Then, the corrupting demons of independence and fear entered, changing the equation of life forever.

However, in the Father's infinite love, the power of their lies has been broken, and the breach caused by the sundering curse healed. The firstborn Son went to the Father to do what the first Adam could not, saying, "Let the curse caused by the enemy fall upon me, that my younger brothers and sisters might live. Bring them back to the Garden. Reinstate them to their position in our family, that they might again have fellowship with you, their Father and mine."

Those who call themselves Christians, therefore, no longer need live under the curse of sin, subject to the lies of the enemy's demons of independence and fear. Jesus took away the curse and revealed the lies for what they are.

Those who follow him and trust him are "taken backward," in a sense, through a spiritual time machine (if such a metaphor can be brought to our aid without demeaning the imperative of the principle) *into the relationship with the Father that existed prior to the Fall.* The apparatus for the accomplishment of this majestic purpose is described in Ephesians 4:8: "When he ascended on high, he led captives in his train."

Having sinned, and recognizing the "wages" of that sin, we are allowed to be cleansed of it and to stand before the Father blameless, guiltless, robed in white.

Such a wonderful, ingenious provision has been made for us by both Father and Son.

In spite of our sin, we have been reinstated into the family of God. The Garden fellowship of Genesis 2 is still ours to enjoy.

We can become his children again!

The Prodigal Son parable precisely describes the process: We had all. We chose to go away and leave everything our Father had provided. To do so was foolish and landed us in despair. However, we may come back. The Father is waiting with open arms and a smile on his face. We have only to admit our foolishness . . . and become again his children.

Jesus was talking about us!

Unknowingly, however, most of us only accept Christ's atonement partially. We dabble his blood scantily upon the doorposts of our heart, just sufficiently to ward off the angel of death. But we do not wash our entire self in the full redemptive power of that blood, sufficient to fully reinstate us into the life of God's family of Genesis 2.

We continue instead to listen to the twin lies.

Though having experienced the "second birth," which Jesus spoke of as the doorway into this spiritual time machine, we still try to do what Adam could not—live in what we call "fellowship" with God while remaining fundamentally independent of his Father-hood in our life.

In other words, positionally we have "gone back" to the Garden . . . but not quite all the way. We have gone back only far enough to enable us to scrape out an existence between Genesis 3:13 and Genesis 3:14.

We have gone back past the curse. Thank God we are free of that! Praise the Lord for the atoning blood of Jesus. Sin no longer has eternal power over us. The angel of death has seen the blood and passed over.

But we have not gone back *past* the lies of inde-pendence and fear that spoke in Genesis 3:4 and 3:10. Those we're still listening to. They clog our ears and blind our eyes with their lies, obscuring the Father from us, just as they did with Adam.

We have not killed the power of independence by choosing to submit in childness to life with the Father.

Instead, we continue to heed the lie—*I alone have the right to be master of my life.*

You can go back to Genesis 3 and have your sins forgiven . . . and still be in fellowship with the serpent and his two lying demons.

Strong words, perhaps, when they fall upon complacent ears—yet true.

Jesus' mission on earth, the reason for the Cross and the purpose for which he descended and then rose with captives in his train, was to take those captives of sin all the way back into *full* fellowship and life with his Father! *All the way back* to Genesis 2 . . . to life in the Father's family *before* the lies.

Unless we get back to Genesis 2, we cannot truly experience intimacy with the Father. Independence and fear will keep us from knowing him rightly.

We must fully immerse ourselves in the redemptive power of his blood, applying it, not niggardly, but enthusiastically.

Applying the brakes and getting off the train of Jesus' ascent prematurely at Genesis 3:13 may protect us from the curse of sin, may get us what is called "saved," and thus qualify us for entry into heaven on the first round; but getting off there will not accomplish the purpose for which Jesus came, for which he died, for which he bore us in his train back to the Father's heart.

The only way for that to be accomplished is to go the full distance with our elder Brother, the firstborn Son—all the way back to the Garden life of Genesis 2. All the way back—beyond the lies and the fig leaves of fear—to the arms of our loving Father!

Such is the pinnacle, the mountaintop, of the Christian faith.

18

LOOKING
BEYOND FEAR

Can you see the high places ahead?

Yes, and now the snows begin to thin again,
as I promised you they would.

Some can see the mountains . . . some will
not yet be able to. But they are there!

As the cautionary voices of independence will
be speaking to you, so too will fear now begin
trying to find ways to disguise his whisperings.
He will never come to you as himself, of course.
You would recognize him too easily. So he will
pretend to be your friend, warning you against
straying too far from the familiar surroundings
of the valley, warning you against moving out
from under the safety of the valley theologies.

But in your deepest heart you know, don't you, that the valley was never really the home where you were meant to dwell. You can feel, can you not, that the Garden life of fellowship is what you were made for.

Do not forsake the journey now that we are so close.

Let us persevere together!

———————

Most of our mistaken notions and misunderstandings concerning God begin with fear. We've kept fear front and center in our incorrect Fatherhood equation.

Fear of God is the chief cause of our unbelief. It is what, more than any other single factor, keeps us from knowing the Father intimately.

After the Cross, fear is to be no more. The lies have been unmasked, their power broken. Paul wrote to Timothy, "God has not given us a spirit of fear." He is not a Father to be hidden from, run from, or feared.

Despite knowing this truth as well as we do, however, most of us continue allowing the rascal called fear to hang around us, misting over our vision with fog from the low places whenever we try to look up toward the Father's face.

Now it is true that the Bible says, "The fear of the Lord is the beginning of wisdom." However, we don't truly understand what this "fear of the Lord" is. Thus, instead of it bringing us wisdom and intimacy with the Father, it keeps us from both.

Fear, to the earthbound senses, results from something dreadfully painful and unpleasant that is to be avoided at any cost. Fear of God, likewise, as experienced by most, has to do with the gnawing sense that God is forever waiting to pounce on us when we do something wrong. Punishment is the inevitable result. So, we begin wrongly, approaching God from a negative perspective.

This is the same lie that the demon fear first told Adam in Genesis 3, and we're still listening to it: "God is going to level his wrath on you the minute he sees you! *Hide from him! It's your only chance.*"

We've got the formula of the Fatherhood equation wrong. Thus, we don't know our Father very well. Nor do we know how properly to "fear" him.

There are two kinds of fear—God's and the demon's.

The fear that properly encourages us toward a relationship with our Father is the fear of Genesis 2:

the fear established by God's design; the loving awe with which we are to honor, respect, and obey him; the fear that is indeed the beginning of wisdom.

"Obey me," says our Father, "so that you will not die. Walk with me, and all I have made is yours."

Such was the command—and the equation for *life*—of Genesis 2.

Genesis 3 fear, on the other hand, is something altogether different. It came, not from the loving Father's heart, but from the pit of hell. It is the fear *of God himself.* It is the lie of fear spoken by Satan's lackey: *Hide from him!* He it is who should be feared—God himself!

If we live in Genesis 3—fearful *of* God—how will we ever learn to walk *with* him in the coolness of the day, rather than trying to hide from him when we hear him coming?

If this lie of fear builds the house of our faith, how can God's Fatherhood find a home there? If the bricks in the walls of our spiritual abode are mortared together with hide-from-him fear, how can they withstand the shaking of the enemy?

Fear can be a normal and healthy thing. God placed fear inside us. He put it there for our protection.

Before he can swim, a child's natural fear of the water protects him from drowning. But once he has learned to swim, that fear is replaced by the capacity to fully enjoy the water, along with a respect for it. He knows, appreciates, and understands the water, its power, and even its danger, but he is no longer frightened of it, nor is he afraid to venture near it.

In the absence of any other response to God, fear is a useful place to begin. Fear is rudimentary, a beginning, a response of spiritual childhood, but something that is cast aside when adulthood comes.

Fear of God's punishment is likewise a response of spiritual childhood—useful for training, as far as it goes, but unable to guide you more than a step or two along the path.

The fear of God *is* the beginning of wisdom. Better to fear God than ignore him.

And there *is* a fear that is appropriate. What we need to fear, however, is the consequences of sin, not the Father who can rescue us from that sin altogether.

Disobeying God indeed does bring fearsome consequences.

A lifetime's independence from him, a lifetime spent ignoring the call of his voice, a lifetime spent pleasing only oneself, a lifetime's disobedience of his commands, a lifetime's sin . . . we do well to tremble at the consequences of such foolishness.

Hell awaits those who persist in ignoring him. Well they ought to fear!

But they should not fear their Father.

He is the one Being they should never fear! *He* is their only possible salvation.

Adam's initial response was correct. He had sinned. He did well to fear.

The fear, however, ought to have been directed at his sin and its consequences, not at the Father. Given what he had done, his Father was his only refuge! He should have run straight *to* him.

Why are we so reluctant to accept the image of the Father that Jesus himself gave? What would have been God's response had Adam run to him instead of fleeing from him in fear . . . run to him to confess his wrong instead of trying to hide it?

We know what it would have been. Did not Jesus himself tell us in Luke 15:18-23?

"I will set out and go back to my father and say to him: Father, I have sinned against heaven and against you. I am no longer worthy to be called your son. . . ." So he got up and went to his father.

But while he was still a long way off, his father saw him and was filled with compassion for him;

he ran to his son, threw his arms around him and kissed him. . . .

The father said to his servants, "Quick! Bring the best robe and put it on him. Put a ring on his finger and sandals on his feet. Bring the fattened calf and kill it. Let's have a feast and celebrate."

Fear is the *beginning* of wisdom, not its end.

O God our Father, why are we so reluctant to accept the image of you that the Son himself gave? Open our eyes to see the exuberant and unreserved love of your Fatherhood! Let us fear our sin, but never you, and may that fear send us running into your loving arms.

19

GOD'S FIRST PURPOSE

At last, as we glance back, we see that the fogs have dissipated. The drifts of snow are only patchy now. It begins to warm. We have indeed come into the first precincts of that region above the snows where the Garden of God's presence sets all things to blooming and flourishing.

Does not the air of this Garden of the Father's begin to feel good, pure, and life-giving to your lungs?

There is, however, one more significant high pathway we must walk, climbing over a bumpy way that is fearsome to many. Indeed, over the years many have sojourned to this very point.

Yet when they encounter this final rocky incline up to the highest plateau—which looks so treacherous and so different from the paths of the valley—the fear of it becomes too much, and many turn back.

Do you wonder how they could come so far and yet not go the rest of the way?

Ah yes, sadly it is true. For we have at last reached the edges of the high mountains themselves, and fear increases his persistent efforts to be heard.

Tighten your hiking boots and take firm hold of your staff.

Once on to the next plateau, the peaks we have long sought will come into view.

———————

One of the greatest weights we must leave behind if we are to scale the heights to reacquaint ourselves with God and know him aright is this: *Knowing the Father may begin with fear, but to know him intimately, the demon's paltry and lying fear must be altogether left behind so that a right and proper Genesis 2 relationship between child and Father may be established.*

The deadly misunderstanding that God's first business is to punish those who do wrong remains one of the most grievous sources of fatal thinking extant in the land. Christians are among those *most* bound by this incorrect point of view. They've gotten off Jesus' reverse salvation train at Genesis 3:13, where the lies of independence and fear still swirl about.

The Father's primary purpose is to reestablish the intimacy of Genesis 2 with his creation, not punish it. If punishment is necessary to accomplish this end, then it is a tool he will make use of, but such is not his primary purpose.

So why *do* we think wrongly about God and his purposes?

First of all, fear is part of our human makeup. We are Adam's offspring too, and the lie that he believed is still being whispered in our ears every day.

Then, theologians have built upon that lie, erecting huge doctrinal edifices upon it: that punishment of sin is God's chief end in the universe, and probably his sole interest in us as well. They have turned truths that are necessary as wall-supports of faith—fear of sin's consequences—into foundations. There's nothing wrong with the construction materials. They've just got them in the wrong place.

We've got fear pointed in the wrong direction—toward the Father instead of toward sin. That's where the lethal error is made that dooms increasing intimacy with God as Father.

The mistake isn't in thinking that God disciplines when it is required. He does. Any loving father would. God *is* bound to deal appropriately with sin, and sin has consequences that must not be ignored.

The mistake comes in drawing the incorrect conclusion that punishment of sin is God's *primary* intent.

One's whole relationship with God, therefore, takes on a negative cast. It is built on fear—the demon's Genesis 3 variety, not God's Genesis 2 brand—rather than on the deeper and more primary characteristics of God's nature.

Today's populist theologians and evangelists have learned to couch this in agreeable ways, double-talking their way into the pleasant-sounding illusion that they are making God's love and goodness supreme. However, at the heart, followed to their logical end point and deepest conclusions, many Christian belief systems are founded on fear—on a response to the punishment that God is required by his nature to mete out upon sinners. Fear of punishment and a desire to avoid

God's retribution remain the bedrock principles un-dergirding their Genesis 3 theologies.

They're still listening to the evil whisper: *Hide from him! It's your only chance.*

They bring Jesus in as the refuge and "hiding place," but the effect is still the same. *Flee from the wrath that is to come!*

Flee *from* God. Flee *to* Jesus. The Son will protect and save us from the Father!

How both Jesus and his Father must be grieved to see the way we have twisted their loving Genesis 2 relationship to fit our Genesis 3 hide-from-him theologies!

Understanding of the Father's being is doomed when Genesis 3 fear is the starting point.

A right and proper Genesis 2 relationship with the Father does not, of course, terminate loving discipline from the hand of the Father. The Bible says he disciplines those he loves. What obedient son or daughter of a loving eternal Father would desire it otherwise? We *want* to grow. How else but through discipline when we require it?

He should not even have to come find us when we need discipline, asking, as he did of Adam and Eve, "Where are you?"

If his loving discipline is needed, the faithful child

should already be running swiftly toward him before he calls!

When we manage to leave the lies of fear behind, whole new worlds of revelation into the Father's being open—including new revelations concerning his discipline, which we can then come to see in the loving way God intends.

20

A GOD TO CALL FATHER

We're high enough above the fogs of the valley now to begin casting our eyes toward the mountaintop estate where our Father dwells.

This high world above the snows, above the cliffs, where the air is clean and purified of the theologies of Genesis 3 fear, is God's home!

Just as we discover the truth about people and situations by watching and listening and asking and conversing and living with them, we can discover the truth about God's character by observing everything about us as we travel! It is the most exciting prospect life has to offer!

We do so by entering into life on his estate, his kingdom. There, by watching and observing and listening and asking, we get to know what the owner of that estate is like.

That is what our journey together is about—discovering the nature of the Father so that we can know him more intimately!

Everything in life mirrors and reflects deeper principles in God's kingdom. All the little clues of discovery we spoke about earlier—they are clues about him. He made every inch of the world, every plant, every flower, every thorn on every rosebush.

Everything—everything—in the world reflects something about God's personality . . . if we have eyes to see all the hidden mysteries of meaning!

The most important mystery of all is this: God is our Father.

He's a Father whose great desire is not to punish us for doing wrong, but to reveal himself to us, his children.

His desire is to share his whole mountaintop estate with us.

He wants us to know him as our Father, as a loving and kind and generous and giving Father who positively delights in his children knowing him.

He wants to walk and visit and fellowship and converse with us in a growing friendship of love.

He's approachable, not distant.

He wants us to call him Father, not think of him as the Awful Powerful Almighty Sovereign of the Universe, Creator of the Heavens, Destroyer of Sin.

He is all those, of course, and much more. There are thousands of aspects and attributes to his character.

But what he wants us to call him is Father.

He wants us to go to him so he can wrap his arms around us and speak to us tenderly and lovingly as his children.

———

Once we're able to look past fear, the remaining fogs disappear and a huge truth becomes visible.

Lay hold of it, and the discovery will be such an adventure that your life will never be the same again!

God is our Father.

Does it not sound singularly unremarkable? We've been talking about that ever since we set out together.

Everybody knows the *words,* knows the *fact* of it.

But very, very few know how to walk in the Fatherness of that central truth.

Why?

Because they're stuck at the point of improper fear—fearing God rather than the consequences of their sin. Therefore, they can't see all his Fatherhood truly entails. Genesis 3 Christianity versus vibrant Genesis 2 intimacy.

The Garden of Genesis 2, the divine and universal "familyhood" of the Creator—that's where he wants us to live . . . with him!

He is a Father exactly as Jesus portrayed in Luke 15, with arms wide open, with a smile on his face, waiting to celebrate life with his creatures.

Jesus told that parable so that we would know what our Father is like!

Such is the wonderful childness into which we may enter in friendship with him. We may share life intimately at every level.

The operative word is *may,* not *must.*

The defining distinction exists in that private region of each of our own wills. He stands patiently, like the father of the prodigal, peering down the road, lovingly hoping for our return.

The decision whether to do so or not is our choice. The Father desperately desires to share such life with us. Through his Son he has made it possible.

Now he awaits our decision.

We are all brothers and sisters, living on this earth together with one common purpose: to discover together as much about the Father of us all as we can . . . and then to go to him so that he may, as Jesus told us, kill the fatted calf and celebrate life with us.

He is our Father, we are his children. Now we have to become *children of childness* by laying aside both our independence and our fear.

He is not an evil Father, intent only on punishing us when we do wrong.

He is a good Father, whose delight is in revealing himself to us.

He is the one good in all the world.

Rather than seeking refuge *from* him because we cower in fear *of* him, we seek refuge *in* him from all the other fears that assail us.

We delight in being with him because he delights in us. And the more we are with him, the more of his being and creation he reveals to us. He is our protector and our friend, our companion and Father—nevermore our fear.

He is a God to call Father.

Ah, Father, what delight you want us to take in finding you so close! Once we apprehend your Fatherhood, how wonderful it is to realize that you are beside us every moment, and that such closeness is not fearsome. You want us to walk with you in the cool of the day, between you and Jesus, our elder Brother. We need have no fear of you, but can delight in being in your presence every moment. You are a Father anxious to smile with us, anxious to speak tenderly to us, anxious to hold us and protect us in your arms.

21

JESUS DID NOT COME TO SAVE US FROM THE FATHER

As we've traversed these pathways higher and higher together, we've been on our way to a great mountaintop estate located up among the peaks ahead. It is the estate where Garden life exists.

We are nearly there!

Now, I know that some of you have heard tales about this place during your years in the valley. Some of you have even heard that the owner of the estate is a giant Ogre intent on killing any trespassers. You've come along this far, but the closer we get, the more worried you become.

It isn't that you want to turn back, because

everything I've told you of this place, and all the glimpses you've already had of it, make it seem like the most wonderful Garden there could ever be. It is literally a land flowing with milk and honey. You want to go there. You might even want to live there.

If only it weren't for the problem of the Ogre you have heard about. If only there was someone to accompany us who would protect us from the Ogre.

Oh, look, my friends! We have arrived at the gate to this high mountain estate. And look! Someone is there to meet us. Perhaps he will protect us.

But he tells us that all the rumors we've heard about the Ogre are untrue. We do not need protection from him. The owner of the estate is really good and loving and kind—in fact, the most wonderful being imaginable.

The guide tells us that he is there to lead us all the way into the center of the estate, showing us all about as we go. He wants to make it

possible for this high mountain region to
become our home!

"Will . . . will you protect us from the owner
if his anger should flare up against us?"
someone asks.

"No. I will take you *to* him; I will not protect
you *from* him."

"But . . . but we thought you were—"

Another shake of his head ends the question.

He assures us once more that he is not there
to protect us from the owner of the estate. He
is going to take us to the owner, assuring us
that he will be all he has promised, and much
more. He is even better than description will
allow!

This guide is none other than Jesus himself,
who has gone on ahead of us, to await our
arrival at the gate to his Father's home!

Jesus came to earth, down to the valley where
we live, to show us his Father, to tell us about
him, to reveal his true nature to us, and then to

**lead us up out of the valley, along the mountain
pathways of discovery, to the very estate of the
King himself!**

———————

Why did Jesus come to earth?

To save the world from its sins?

Jesus did die, of course, and he did save us from our
sins. Such was intrinsic to the Father's purpose.

Such was not, however, the central purpose of his
mission.

Let us ask another question. Why was it necessary
for Jesus to save us from our sins?

To keep us from the fires of hell?

To answer yes makes avoiding hell and being saved
from God's punishment of sin the chief reasons for
Jesus' coming.

Again, Jesus does save from hell, and he does atone
for sin, but such was not his primary purpose in
coming to earth.

Sadly, a great many of those calling themselves
Christians view Jesus' mission on earth as being sent to
protect us from certain death at the hand of the Ogre
waiting to kill us because of our sin. That is how most

prevailing evangelical theologies interpret the Atonement and Jesus' death on the cross.

Though this is not explicitly stated, the implication is that Jesus saves us *from God* almost more than he saves us from our sins.

God cannot be both loving Father and avenging Ogre at the same time. He can display a wide variety of seemingly disparate characteristics in his complex nature. But his intrinsic being must be *one*.

It's the dichotomy between Genesis 2 and Genesis 3. It's the chasm between Garden fellowship and the lie crying *Hide!*

Jesus didn't come primarily to save us from the avenging hand of a terrible Ogre. In essence, Jesus came so he could tell us:

Your sins are going to result in your death. But your Father loves you so much that he has sent me down to you so that I could lead you back up here . . . to him! I cannot *myself* save you. I am merely the Son. I have come to fetch you and take you home. The Father has sent me for you . . . because of his great love for you. *He* is your salvation and refuge. I am the one he sent to offer you *his* salvation. He alone, your tender and loving Father, can save you from your sins!

Come, take my hand, let me show you your wonderful and loving Father. Don't hide from him. Come *to* him . . . with me.

That was Jesus' purpose in coming to earth: to reveal God's personality and character, and to lead us to the Father, so that the Son and the Father *together* might save us from our sins.

God is our Father.

Jesus came to show us and tell us what he is like. These are the words he spoke, which reveal the manner of the Father's Fatherness:

His father saw him and was filled with compassion for him; he ran to his son, threw his arms around him and kissed him. . . .

The father said to his servants, "Quick! Bring the best robe and put it on him. Put a ring on his finger and sandals on his feet. Bring the fattened calf and kill it. Let's have a feast and celebrate."

Father, forgive us for believing so comfortably the lies of the demon of fear, even more than we have believed in your goodness. Forgive us for glossing over the words of your Son, Jesus: "I and the Father are one." Forgive us for erecting a schism in the very

Godhead of your being itself, as if it were the Son's duty to protect us from the Father he so loves! Forgive us our foolish blindness that would pit Jesus against you!

Thank you for at last opening our eyes to the truth that Jesus wants to take us to you, in whom is our salvation, not hide us from your wrath behind his atonement. Forgive us for so long living in the midst of this schism created by our unbelief.

Help us to see, dear Father, that independence and fear—and all the evil hosts like them that Satan sends against us—are the enemies we need to be saved from! Sin is the enemy, not you, our precious loving Father!

Truly we need rescuing, and you are the one who can save us!

Jesus doesn't save us from you. He brings us to you, so that you can save us! Father and Son together pull us out of the evil pit of independence into which we have fallen.

Open our eyes still more, Father. Reveal more of the high purposes of your truth to us.

Help us to cast off the futile fig leaves of our fear and run to you, confessing ourselves the foolish children we are. Surround us with the warmth and

*love of your embrace. Keep us from succumbing to
the lies of independence and fear ever again.*

Help us to become fully mature children indeed.

*God, O God our Father, help us to believe in
your smiling, open-armed goodness . . . and that
you love us!*

PART V
HOME AMONG
THE PEAKS

———

Scaling the Heights

22

How Big Is Our God?

Our journey thus far has been a rugged climb toward the high reaches of understanding God's purposes. No doubt many of you have some bruises to show for it, and our company is probably smaller than it was.

Those of you who remain, are you ready to move on still higher? The path grows no less steep, nor is the way more traveled. We are bound where few souls have trod.

Take heart, however, for the way is not as dangerous as it seems. We are within the borderlands of the King's estate now. We have been met by Jesus at the gate and invited further upward and deeper in.

In leaving fear behind, we have crossed a
great threshold and are now inside the fences of
the vast land about which we have heard so
much, and for sight of which we left the valley
below.

No one falls from these heights; they are only
strengthened from the vigorous climbs.

Ah, and the air begins to grow so clean, so
fresh! The fortifying energy of it increases,
while the sting begins to lessen. Can you not
already sense the difference in your spiritual
lungs?

Look around. Then take in a deep breath and
exhale slowly with pleasure. Do you not feel
your chest expanding and filling with greater
capacity than before? Doesn't it feel good!

The air of Fatherhood is rich air!

It is the air our soul was made to breathe. If it
takes a rugged climb and some bumps against
the shins and knees of our prior-held traditions,
is that not a small price to pay to feel that rich

oxygen of Fatherhood life expanding to new places within us?

Do you not begin to sense, too, the filling of that empty reservoir of longing within your heart? Are not the waters of the Father's being already trickling their way into that inner cistern, giving you hope that it will never be parched and dry again?

As good as they feel, however, these are only the first trickles! We have not yet arrived at that fountainhead at the core of the mountain from which the waters gush with never diminishing supply.

Let us be bold to strike on, then, toward intimacy with the Father of our Brother Jesus! Let us continue steadily upward, with Jesus as our guide.

He went to the hills to seek his Father. Now he has brought us with him to those same mountain places.

Let us pursue our course . . . upward!

As we go, there is one clear marker that will make the way plain before us. We will even be able to continue on in the darkness if we heed its words: Discover more about your Father.

We may talk and converse with the Father, as children do when their own smiling and loving fathers look upon their faces. Oh, how his heart is eager to open itself fully and completely to us and give us room therein to live with him!

Genesis 2 fellowship is what the Father wants us to seek with him.

———

Two operative words revealing how big God's Fatherhood is, while at the same time preventing most people from fathoming one-trillionth of its reality, are the words *utterly* and *everything*.

Christians living on the borderlands of the valley know that God loves them. They don't, however, really know (in their hearts!) that he loves them *utterly*.

Valley Christians know in small measure that God does what he can to reveal his love and that he desires relationship with them. They are reluctant, however, to recognize that he will do *everything* possible to cause that to happen.

Noted British scholar J. B. Phillips wrote a book whose title contributes as much to the quest after Fatherhood as the content of the book itself: *Your God Is Too Small.* Dozens of times I have turned those simple words upon myself in the realization that my faithlessness at some point stemmed from the fact that I was attempting to place my trust in a lowercase god.

How do I view the two words *utterly* and *everything?*

Do I really believe in an uppercase God? Does God love me *utterly?* Will God do *everything* possible to reveal that love?

How big is the God/god we trust and believe in?

What might be the implications if we took these words at face value and really believed that God not just loved us, but loved us *utterly* . . . that he not merely desires a relationship with us, but can and will do *everything* to bring that about?

How BIG are we willing to believe God is?

These are far-reaching questions to examine, with huge implications . . . if the words *utterly* and *everything* are truly where the answers lie.

Not only how big are we willing to believe, but how big might we *dare* think the Father is! How far might we be bold enough to think his loving Father-hood will extend?

Are we willing to bring the imaginations of his creation in at this point to stretch our faith in the utter-everything–ness of his Fatherhood?

Some will be afraid to do so.

God has not, however, given us a spirit of fear, but of loving boldness!

The best way to learn of the Father is to listen to what Jesus said and then ask for his help. He is our elder Brother. This is the purpose for which he came to earth, and he eagerly awaits our asking. If Jesus came to show us the Father, then let us allow him to do just that.

> *Spirit of Truth, Jesus our Brother, we ask for your help in this quest we are on. We have prayed for the Father to reveal himself to us, to open the eyes of our heart and mind to see him as he truly is. Now we ask you also to reveal truth to our innermost parts.*
>
> *As we read of your life on earth, illuminate the eyes of our understanding to see the Father's being and character in your words, in what you did, in what you were constantly teaching your disciples. Turn us to your life, as written by your servants Matthew, Mark, Luke, and John. Open our eyes to*

their words more fully. Open us to the Fatherhood of their message.

O Lord our Savior and Friend and Brother, reveal to us more and more what you meant when you said that if we have seen you, we have seen the Father.

23
FOLLOW
FATHERHOOD
TO FINALITY

As we strike out toward the very center of the King's estate, the air continues to grow more rarified.

Some will turn back, even now, even after tasting these first vitalizing draughts.

But have courage, my friend, our Guide and elder Brother will not lead us astray!

And not only is Jesus with us and leading us, but the Father too is right beside us—ready to reveal himself every moment as we focus our eyes to see him. Intimacy, not remoteness, is his desire.

We are journeying within his regions now, and though we may not always be aware of him,

> he is our constant companion—even closer to
> our hearts than Jesus. As much as he loves us,
> Jesus can never come as close as the Father, for
> he did not create us. We were born in the same
> place as was his divine Sonship—in the Father's
> loving heart!

Even though the words *Follow Fatherhood to Finality* are contrived, they speak an enormous truth.

If the sons and daughters of God's family fully apprehended the simple fact that we could follow the Fatherhood of God all the way to finality, all the way back to a Genesis 2 relationship, the world may well have been redeemed centuries ago.

Men and women are so desperately hungry for true Fatherhood, and we children of his family have been entrusted to take it to them.

Alas, *we* do not know the fullness of God's Fatherhood either; and, saddest of all, many of us who live right in his family are not hungry to discover it!

Before us, therefore, is the vital question: How do we break the shells and peel away the husks that enclose truths about God so that we can get all the way *inside* them, where dwells intimacy with the Father?

God's Fatherhood *cannot* be experienced and known and discovered—and lived in—at an external level. That is impossible.

Discovery has to begin by going higher, as we follow some of the things on our "list" of God's attributes out to the end to see what they really imply.

A key foundation stone in the writings of two of this century's renowned exponents of the faith—Francis Schaeffer and C. S. Lewis—was their insistence that people must look at the logical conclusions of their own words: If I say I believe such-and-such, then what is the practical implication of that belief when it is followed all the way out to its ultimate and logical conclusion?

The value of such logical-consequence thinking is that it forces you to make a foundational evaluation concerning the veracity of your belief system. Can you, or can you not, live by your beliefs? Do they hold up even when you follow them all the way out to the end?

For example, if I live in the Sahara I might say, "I do not believe in rain." But what are the logical consequences of such a statement? What do I do when I travel to Scotland and find myself in the middle of a downpour? If I am an honest man, I have to reevaluate my belief system, realizing that it cannot hold up when applied beyond my own small, protected environment.

Both Lewis and Schaeffer argued with enormous analytical insight and power that when you follow various philosophical explanations of the universe out to the logical conclusions inherent in their presuppositions, the Christian faith is the *only* one truly consistent with the nature of man and the universe as they actually exist. Every other worldview breaks down eventually.

You may devise your own private little Sahara and a worldview that explains everything to your satisfaction, but somewhere else on the planet it is going to rain, and where is your worldview then?

Consistency. That is the key.

Can you *live* on the basis of what you say you believe—no matter where you take those beliefs, no matter what they come up against?

This is enormously significant, for the inconsistent cannot be true. A philosophical position that is inconsistent—that we cannot live out in practice at the logical extension of its fundamental suppositions—is a philosophical position that *cannot* be true.

Schaeffer's and Lewis's insistence on this exercised profound impact on both non-Christians and Christians during this century. Non-Christians flocked to listen to Schaeffer. Lewis was even on the cover of *Time* magazine. The world listened because, despite the inconsistency of most of the positions they hold, people generally place a value on common sense and reasonable thinking.

Both men were admired even by those who disagreed with them, because they could see that the minds of these two Christian thinkers were keen and that they were honest and sincere in their desire to communicate truth.

In light of this, however, it is curious and disturbing to realize how little Christians have sought to move to finality *inside* the doctrines of faith. We have not trained ourselves to think with logic, reason, insight, and common sense.

We admire it outside the wall, where the intellectual battle is waged with the unbelieving world by Christian apologists. We love to watch men like Lewis take a Sahara-desert philosopher to the middle of a rain forest and douse the irrationality of his worldview. We love to see non-Christians put in their place, as it were, for the illogic between supposition and conclusion. But we are loath to look at such holes *within* our *own* thought systems.

Why is it that among the masses within evangelical Christianity a high premium is not generally placed on the kind of commonsense, logical, clearheaded, and rational thinking that so distinguished Francis Schaeffer and C. S. Lewis?

Following our suppositions out to their logical conclusions is an exercise many are utterly unacquainted with. The whole concept, in fact, is probably unknown to 90 percent of those considering themselves followers of Christ.

It is as important to follow things to the end *inside* the Christian faith as *outside* it. Christians, to be effective and consistent believers, need to look at the doctrines and beliefs they hold and follow *them* all the way out to their logical conclusions to see if they make sense in the final analysis.

Not only to see if they "make sense," but, even more important, to see if they can live consistently on the basis of what they say they believe.

This is no mere mental exercise. There is an imperative urgency to living consistently with what I say I believe, all the way out to where logical extension meets conclusion. If I say I believe something, can that belief intellectually, scripturally, consistently hold up . . . or does it break down, like a thundershower over the head of a Sahara theologian.

Can my beliefs be consistently lived by?

Not enough Christians have been asking this question from *within* the body of Christ, inquiring whether certain tenets we have long assumed to be true can, in fact, be supported out at the end point of their extension.

It is fearfully easy to live inconsistently with the precepts of our faith, dwelling at the edges of the valley, refusing to venture, because of the rigors of the climb, to the mountains.

That is why it has taken so long for us to get to this point in our journey. Now, however, we have reached the point at which we must break open our previously limited understanding so that we may move to the heights of God's Fatherhood.

How do we get inside the husks . . . how do we live by the truths we discover . . . how do we scale at last the highest pinnacles of faith?

How? *By following the principles and attributes of God's Fatherhood to finality,* by extending the suppositions that we say we believe all the way out to their logical conclusions.

This statement is anything but *merely* intellectual. It is one of the most practical things any of us will ever do.

O God, help our faith to be real and true and consistent . . . all the way out to the farthest end points of what we say we believe!

24

DO WE REALLY BELIEVE IN GOD'S FATHERHOOD?

Finally, we have arrived at the doorway to intimacy!

This is where the quest to discover the character and Fatherhood of God begins to approach the mountain peaks!

And look! Do you see those faint footsteps in the rocky way before us? They are the imprint of Jesus' steps!

He met us at the gate. He reassured us that the Father he is taking us to meet is no Ogre. And he is leading the way before us.

That is why I can speak with such boldness when I say that the way we are heading toward the highest mountain regions of all is a way where there is no ultimate danger, only glorious and refreshing new airs and waters of life!

Let us press on, then, upward, higher toward the heart, the nucleus, the living Center of the estate!

———

To grasp God's Fatherhood in the dynamic way that will change our "acquaintance" with him into a *knowing* of intimacy, we first have to find out whether we really believe what we say about him.

Most of what we might call the "attributes" of God's Fatherhood are familiar to us all. Given sixty seconds, we could each no doubt list fifteen or twenty. We all have a ready-made informational composite we could recite almost as quickly as the multiplication table.

We know these attributes fairly well because they have been emphasized in our Sunday school classes and Bible studies, and we've heard them from the pulpit.

The problem isn't that we don't know what God's Fatherhood *is*. The problem is that we don't know how to live *in* the reality of that Fatherhood.

So there will be no such list provided here.

It is infinitely better to apprehend *one* truth of

God's being—a *full* truth, a "live" truth—and apprehend it all the way to its core, and then live in the reality of that discovery, than to know ten thousand facts about God and not live in them.

Infinitely better!

Gathering intellectual information is a pointless exercise in the spiritual realm. If this inner journey means anything in your life, I pray it means you have been helped to *live* in what you know, whether that be one truth or the entire scope of Fatherhood.

It's a process of discovery no one can do for you, for it is personal and internal.

Even Jesus had to go through this process of discovery. What was he doing in the temple at age twelve? He had already embarked on the quest to know his Father.

How did he spend the years between twelve and thirty? Sometime during that period his earthly father, Joseph, died. Since there was certainly great love between them, can you not imagine Jesus wrestling through his relationship with his Father in heaven vis-à-vis his relationship with Joseph?

Jesus didn't merely float onto the scene in the first chapter of Mark at thirty years of age. He was a living, breathing, thinking, feeling human being. What did the Temptation in the wilderness entail? Jesus was probing the limits of his Father's goodness and trust-worthiness.

He had to KNOW his Father. Anything less than the *full* knowledge that his Father was good and could be utterly trusted, and Jesus might have returned to the safety of Galilee when the moment of ultimate trial came in Gethsemane.

He had to go through the process of discovery and then take that personal, intimate knowing of the Father and live by it—and die by it—all the way to the end . . . to finality.

Jesus had to travel the uncertain paths to the mountaintops of Fatherhood too.

He is our example.

Jesus followed every one of the attributes of his Father to finality: at twelve, in his youth, after Joseph died, as he worked in the carpenter's shop providing for his family, in the desert with Satan and the animals and the angels, in the Garden, on the cross, in the tomb, in the very depths of hell itself, and on the first Easter morning.

He KNEW his Father!

That's how I want to know the Father too!

It is to such a wondrous search that I have dedicated my life. When I read those magnificent words in

John 17:20-26, I find myself swallowed up and taken *inside* that prayer! It moves me beyond description!

Jesus prayed . . . for *me!*

He prayed that I would know his Father!

Can you imagine! I hunger with a longing I cannot describe to yield myself so fully to the purposes of God that he can indeed fulfill Jesus' words in my life!

Oh, to be part of the answer to that mighty prayer! The very thought of it is more wonderful than the human mind can comprehend!

25

DISCOVERING WHETHER GOD IS REALLY GOOD

Look up, my fellow travelers! Look up and behold a great yet astonishingly simple truth that a white-bearded stranger helped me lay hold of many years ago.

The truth is just this—the Father is good!

Astonishing, you say. How so? It is so elementary as to scarcely be worth mentioning.

Ah, so I thought too, for I had been well taught in the valley theologies . . . until that venerable friend helped open my inner eyes to see the great truth of GOODNESS.

Indeed, it is because of this truth that the air up here is so clean and vital. It is goodness that allows you to see with such clarity and

bound up these high pathways with such
vigor.

Goodness is the very oxygen of the place!

How such an elemental truth could have
caused such trepidation in my soul, I can now
scarce imagine. How grateful I am that the
white-bearded one brought me out of those
valley fogs and showed me about this pleasant
land, teaching me to breathe its invigorating air
. . . as I am now bringing you.

Breathe, my friends . . . breathe the air of
goodness!

———

Most believers would say, "Of course God is good."

When adversity comes, however, what do you and
I do? Ordinarily we do not rejoice. When suffering
comes, we grumble and grouse and complain.

Do you see how down-to-earth and practical this
is?

If we truly believe the Father is good, and believe
that he is always doing his very best for his creatures,
and if his goodness is truly one of the central truths of

our whole being, then we will *know* all is well—in the midst of any and all adversity.

We *will* rejoice.

The Father's goodness will be a truth we live in *all* the way, *out to the end,* even in the midst of suffering. When circumstances appear "bad," we know otherwise. All the way to finality. When the rains come, they do not douse our Sahara theologies because our belief system is consistent at the end point no matter what comes.

Suffering, crisis, heartache, natural disaster, even death abound in this world. Yet there resides in the depths of our soul a calm serenity and quietude. We know that God is still good—all the way to the end, to finality . . . absolutely . . . utterly . . . no matter what.

For the mature Christian, some of this outlook is hinted at. Yes, there exists a peace, even in dark circumstances, that the world is unacquainted with.

Yet, when faced with the horrible, cruel, unjust suffering that we witness in the world around us, would we not all admit to places in our consciousness where we find ourselves "wondering" about the totality of God's goodness?

Certainly I have to make such an admission.

When I see the world's heartbreaking grief, the starving and dying all over our planet, the homeless, the innocent victims of crime, the modern scourge of abortion, the devastation of war, I *have* wondered.

I've wrestled through the question of how far God's goodness extends—wrestled it through in depth when reading about some of what he told the Israelites to do in the Old Testament.

I wrestled with it two weeks ago when the body of a young woman of our family's acquaintance was found brutally murdered by a teenage gang. As long as I have been walking with the Lord, I suddenly found myself having to wrestle through the most fundamental issue of all—the extent of God's love. How could I, who believed in the limitlessness of God's love and goodness, frame a meaningful response to the girl's stunned parents?

I've wondered many times where the end point, where the limit is to God's goodness.

It *is* difficult to follow a *good* Fatherhood all the way to finality. At some point, for every one of us, that goodness begins to break down. The rain begins to fall, and we find our belief system facing the ultimate test.

I've succumbed, as I'm sure all of you have, to the persistent human tendency to reduce God's goodness to the finite regions where my mind can figure it out, where I can box it up and define it and understand it.

How else do we deal with the seeming inconsistencies of the Old Testament and the cruelty and pain and suffering that exists in the world?

It's a conundrum of epic proportions.

We either engage in this intellectual tug-of-war at the foundation point of belief, or we glibly retreat into the intellectual dishonesty of unthinkingness, saying, "Well, God's ways are higher than man's ways . . . that's not for me to understand."

If we're capable of serious thought at all, and if we're honest with ourselves, we *do* limit God to our finite capacity to understand.

But the minute we do, we lessen our capacity to truly *know* him . . . as he is! We shrink him to fit *our* mentality, rather than stretching ourselves past the husk, past the shell, into the high reaches of his infinite being and character.

One of the key steps, therefore, In the process of "discovering" how to live in God's Fatherhood does not involve memorizing a list of traits, but discovering what those attributes really *mean* when followed all the way out to the end.

All the way!

Someone's telling you "God is good," therefore, won't enable you to know and live in the truths of Fatherhood.

Goodness at that point is just a word representing

the husk or shell enclosing an attribute most of us would have to admit we still do not grasp very clearly all the way out at the end point where suffering and cruelty slam up against it.

There are, of course, all sorts of theological shadow dances around such difficulties. But many of them make as much sense as the emperor's invisible robes, and with similar result. We delude only ourselves with theological double-talk. The world is not fooled for a minute. Which is one reason why, for the most part, it's not paying much attention.

To know and live in God's goodness requires the following of that *goodness* out to finality to find out whether you *really* believe that the Father is good—in your brain, in your heart, in all your thoughts and attitudes and beliefs and relationships and decisions, in how you view Scripture, in how you respond to the world . . . in everything!

Now we're beginning to scale the true high mountains of faith where intimacy begins to be the reward of those who diligently seek him!

When we start living and believing what we *say* we believe, indeed the world will take notice!

———————

A profound truth was revealed to me nearly twenty

years ago when my wife and I were visiting with a friend who had just returned from L'Abri in Switzerland.

A calm was evident in his carriage, a new maturity. Judy asked him, "If you had to boil it down to one thing you learned from your time at L'Abri, what would it be?"

Our friend was quiet for a long time. Very thoughtful. The air hung heavy with silent expectation. It was obviously a huge, encompassing question for him.

When he finally spoke, his voice was quiet, but so earnest, with a quality of solidity and tenderness and love. His words carried a Rock of Gibraltar strength.

"That God is good," he replied.

None of the three of us said anything for a long time. We merely sat soaking in the depth and implication of his answer.

That single word *good* rang with such quiet force and power that I have never forgotten the moment.

Those four words have been with Judy and me ever since.

Our friend had been a Christian for years—a solid, growing Christian. He had spent the past months studying, learning, reading. He had probably learned five hundred new things about his Christian faith.

But it all reduced down to one single element of

God's Fatherhood, which he no longer knew merely intellectually. He had gotten hold of it at a profoundly deeper level, and it had changed him . . . forever.

He had peeled off the husk of the thing called God's "goodness" and had found out in a deeply personal way about the life that was contained in the seed inside.

The high-mountain truth.

The *live* truth that *is* God's goodness!

That is what we're talking about.

To *live,* you've got to crack the shell and get inside . . . where God put the life.

That's what our friend discovered at L'Abri. He'd known about the shell for years. He'd probably even pecked and chipped away at the outer enclosure before that, maybe even had a hole or two knocked out so that he could hold his eye up and squint to see what was inside the egg.

But at L'Abri the shell broke wide open, and life came pouring out!

PART VI

THE INNER
CHAMBER WHERE
THE FATHER'S
HEART DWELLS

Finding at Last

Our Eternal

Dwelling Place

26

THE THREE MOUNTAIN PEAKS OF FATHERHOOD

In the high places of faith, the husks and shells and outer casings in which truth comes to the residents of the valley all vanish and fall away. There are no hidden things on the mountaintops. Here, where Jesus said all will be made known, truth is plainly visible! And life in the mountains is lived by partaking every moment of living truth!

We have come now to a new plateau of our climb, that for which we have been preparing with every prior step. From it, the pinnacle of our quest will soon become visible.

Hear me well, my fellow travelers. This pinnacle I speak of is no apex of information, no pot of gold climaxing our quest, which will cause you to exclaim, "Aha! So this is the summum bonum, the 'greatest thing' concerning God's Fatherhood!"

No. A more quiet and pensive experience awaits you—a slowly dawning revelation that will unfold within you like the unfurling frond of a new fern, gradually revealing more and more of its color and magnificence.

We have been getting ourselves ready all this time, not so much turning over new ground as spading the hard soil of our existing beliefs so that our life will at last be capable of growing those plants and bearing that fruit intended for it.

We have been climbing, yes, but not so that we will get high enough to see altogether new outlooks. Our intent is not to seek some new theology, some new brand of spirituality, some new way of viewing God's Fatherhood.

Instead, we have been preparing our eyes to

behold greater heights—with new insight—that enable us to look more deeply into truths we have known all along. In other words, our journey has equipped us for a new level of seeing.

Having scaled these heights of preparedness, we now reach that pinnacle where we can look back and see the very mountains whose summits were obscured through the valley mists below.

The same mountains . . . beheld anew!

Our journey, our climb, has been preparational, not informational.

Climbing past these initial plateaus has been necessary because they have led us ever upward, following the footsteps of Jesus toward the heights we have now reached.

Suddenly so much is visible . . . in every direction!

As we cast our gaze upward from this new vantage point, we behold three enormous mountain peaks. These are the heights toward which we have been journeying. They represent the summits of the Father's being and character, which we are now prepared to see in all their glory.

The first is the tallest; the others stand just slightly lower and to each side. These are truths whose foothills and surrounding husks we have long been familiar with:

God the Father is LOVE.

God the Father is GOOD.

God the Father is TRUSTWORTHY.

Many lesser peaks dot the horizon of our view in many directions, but these tower above the rest.

God desires his people to take these three eternal and powerful truths into their innermost being and live inside them every moment.

And there, nestled at the point where these three peaks converge, lies the mansion of the Father's estate! And from its innermost chamber flow forth the waters of life.

It is here he desires us to make our home and thus fulfill our personhood . . . and our destiny.

Do we dare move forward still farther?

Do we trust Jesus' word that his Father is utterly and completely good and that there is nothing whatever we need fear from him?

Strengthen our heart, Father of Jesus. We desire to

press forward all the way. But the air is so new to breathe. Help us, we pray!

Lead us to the center of your home, where you would have your family dwell with you.

27

THE HEART
CHAMBER OF LIFE

Tentatively, as Jesus gently leads us onward, we venture upward within the three peaks themselves where sits the Father's home.

We gasp at the sight!

It is not only glorious to behold but is homey and inviting and comfortable looking.

Still Jesus encourages us forward through the door of the magnificent mansion and into the inner chambers.

There, to our amazement, we find the Father himself! And wonder of wonders, he is just as Jesus has been telling us all this time.

One look into his smiling, loving, Fatherly face tells us he is not the Fearsome Sovereign

we thought no man could look upon lest he
die. He is the Father of the prodigal—
watching and waiting for us! We have been
expected! His face is so full of love, how can
we look anywhere else in all the universe!
How could we not have seen the love that was
radiating from him all along?

———————

Speechless, we approach the Father's presence, unable still, after all Jesus has said, to keep from timorousness, though the expression of love on his face dissipates the last lingering shadows of valley fear remaining.

Both the Father and Jesus are smiling broadly, unreserved in their happiness to bring us inside with them and share all their divine familyhood with us. It feels so good to be wanted, to be loved, to know that they both desire an intimate relationship with us . . . all the time, in everything, and forever!

We know now this is where we belong!

This is the place for which we have hungered, even without knowing it, all our life!

The quest of our heart, our mind, our soul, our will has reached its culmination, its final destination!

Jesus leads us straight to the Father, then places our hand in his.

Henceforth, Jesus says, *just as I instructed my disciples to do, you are to call him Abba . . . Daddy . . . Father!*

Now at last the Father himself speaks.

His voice is nothing like what we have expected. It is neither thunderous nor loud, neither stern nor reproving. It is the tenderest, kindest, most soothing and loving, most Fatherly voice we could ever imagine. It is a strong and resonant voice, but strong with invitation, not reproach. The very sound, as the words fall from his lips, makes us want to run into his arms and jump into the lap of his embrace, nevermore to leave!

You may make your home here, the Father says, *in these innermost rooms of the palace of my presence. Here, in this very place . . . with me. I WANT you to live here with me. It is your choice, of course. Many of my sons and daughters do not choose to live here, but I hope you will. That is why I sent my servant down to the valley to bring you to my Son, who has now brought you here to me, that I might show you myself. Come!*

Still holding our hand, the Father now leads us farther inside. Walking between him and Jesus, we find ourselves entering a huge room more magnificent than imagination can describe. Even though we thought we had seen the extent of the mansion as we approached from the outside, now we see instantly how mistaken we were, for in all directions we are able to see no wall of boundary anywhere. The inside of the chamber seems to go on without end.

Knowing our thoughts, the Father speaks.

This is the chamber where my love, goodness, and trustworthiness dwell. And you are correct: There are no walls herein, for the room extends forever in all directions. This is the heart of the mansion of my presence, the heart of my very being itself. This is where I invite all my sons and daughters to dwell with me.

As he says the words, for the first time the smile leaves the Father's face, but only for a moment. Then he says, *Come in still farther. I have more to show you.*

Now he leads us toward a great fountain in the distant center of the room, where mighty waters spring up thundering from deep within the earth where no eye can see. A massive emerald green pool of unfathomable depth extends around the spring, out of which emanate innumerable streams and rivers and brooks of varying size and swiftness, flowing off in a hundred directions.

All the legends of green springs and brooks flowing throughout the mountains are true!

Again, knowing our thoughts, the Father answers.

The waters of my life flow out from here, from my heart of love, to all the earth, to all the corners of my estate.

Even to the valley? we ask.

Yes. No one, even in the valley, could live an instant without the nourishment of these waters, though they know it not, nor do they have the faintest inclination where they originate.

Why don't you tell them?

Ah, my child, I am constantly telling them, in a thousand ways. My Son has told them. My servants through the ages have told them. Everything I have made tells them—shouts to them—of these waters and these high mountains where I beckon them. . . . Look! Then come! These waters give life to the whole earth, and I have placed hints of these waters, tiny pictures of myself, reminders of the home of this chamber, small sounds of my voice, into everything I have made. I am constantly encouraging them to SEE and HEAR in a thousand ways. But alas, it is wearying work for my Son and my Spirit to open their eyes and unplug their ears.

We are thankful you were so patient with us, we find ourselves saying, and that you brought us here.

I desire that you make your dwelling with me, the Father says, smiling broadly. *Come . . . drink of the waters of my being, my very divine self, my love. For this you came . . . now drink.*

We stoop down and set our lips to the green pool of Life.

The water is like nothing we have ever tasted!

With the first sip, suddenly we feel the refreshing springs of living water filling to overflowing every once-thirsty reservoir within us.

The water you are drinking is the water of my love, which is the essence of my very self, the Father says. *Only the waters from this spring satisfy all thirsts, in all hearts, removing all cares, and bringing peace in all things. Henceforth, this is to be the divine well of your sustenance, of your very life.*

28

LIVING IN THE THREEFOLD HEART OF THE ESTATE

We try to take in all the Father says, but it is still new—and so different from what we learned about the Father of Jesus in the valley assemblies where a different path toward spirituality was taught.

"This is to be your home forevermore," the Father now tells us. "This room is the place prepared just for you, and for all the offspring of my heart. This is where my family dwells—my Son, my Spirit, my children, as well as myself.

"Here, in the chamber of my love, my goodness, and my trustworthiness are the source of all life itself. This is the room from which my I-AM–ness springs . . . and here will you be with me

forever.

"I love you. I will accomplish nothing but
good in your life. You may trust me.

"Make yourself at home here . . . in my heart
of love."

––––––––––

The most basic truth in all the universe, lying open in
the pages of Scripture for all to see, the foundation for
the very kingdom of God itself, the foundation for *all*
existence throughout *all* creation, is nothing more nor
less than this: God really is just what the Bible says of
him—he is *love.*

In only one passage throughout all of God's Word
does any biblical writer take it upon himself to fully
define God's being. You know where it is. The writer
was the disciple whom Jesus loved.

Who is God? What is he like? What are the attributes of his vast personality and character? What is the
summation of his being?

John told us near the end of his first letter: *God is
love.*

Many, many other aspects combine to make up the

full and rounded multifaceted breadth of his character. But all are subservient to that great high-mountain defining truth that what he *is,* is love!

This is the highest summit of his being.

Just behind it, and only slightly lower, stand the truths of goodness and trustworthiness so intrinsic to love.

All other attributes of his infinite being—hundreds of other characteristics . . . thousands of them!—are swallowed up within the magnitude of these three.

These are the guiding principles of Genesis 2 life with the Father, which Jesus came to earth to lead us toward, that we might again participate in full Garden fellowship with him.

It is these three we are to live *in,* as we walk the high mountain regions with our Father . . . to *live inside* of.

These truths, because they characterize and thus *comprise* the Father's heart, are to be our home. Such was God's plan from the beginning.

Are they just too good to be true?

No. *They are just so good they must be true!*

Father, forgive us our unbelieving and untrusting heart! Why can we not bring ourselves to believe that you, our Father, really are good.

Oh, but if you are God, if you are love, then how could you be other than good?

Why is it so hard for us to trust you absolutely and completely to be loving and good . . . all the way to the most difficult places . . . all the way into the deepest and most hidden corners of our own self?

Throw aside the coverings, throw wide the cellar doors of our being! Invade every inch, illuminate us everywhere with the probing light of your truth-searching Spirit.

Fill the reservoirs and cisterns within us with the waters of your precious self! It is to know you that we have undertaken this journey. Fill us, we pray you, to overflowing . . . only with you!

Help us, O God, our good, loving, and trust-worthy Father. Reveal yet more of your truth and your being to us.

Now that we have arrived at your mountain estate, where your mansion is and where the waters of your life gush forth to fill us and where you yourself live, oh, help us now, more than ever, to call you Father!

29

A CONVERSATION
WITH THE SON

Our first days and weeks in the mansion of
the Father's love, goodness, and trustworthiness
are wondrous beyond measure as we enjoy his
presence, drink of those waters that for so long
we have thirsted, and call him Father with the
abandonment of the Abba-delighted child.

But gradually new questions begin to present
themselves.

From out of the distant past, when we still
lived in the valley, precepts and teachings deeply
ingrained begin once more to intrude upon our
thoughts, reminding us that the Father's estate
is much larger than this magnificent mansion
whose inner chambers are so pleasant.

As we look around us, we begin to notice a great many others about, moving to and fro. They are carrying containers of great variety.

The rooms of the mansion have not seemed crowded, we think to ourselves. Where do all these people live? And what is it they are about?

Our elder Brother has already noticed our concern. One morning, therefore, he bids us rise early and accompany him out into the distant regions of the estate. Along the way he tells us what we are going to see.

———————

Our Father's estate, Jesus tells us, *is of far vaster extent than many imagine. Its reaches are immense—limitless by measurement known to mortal man.*

Is there no end to it?

It is said there is, Jesus replies with a smile. *But the Father has not revealed all things even to me, and where those limits may be, even I do not know.*

What about the limitations of man's devising? we wonder, remembering the disquiet we have been feeling for several days.

Again a smile comes to Jesus' face, although one tinged with sadness.

There are many such, he says slowly, *and they grieve our Father.*

Does he make no limits, draw no ultimate lines, fix no end points?

Oh yes. There are borders to his land.

Where then?

They're not meant for mortals to see. He pauses, as if remembering fondly a conversation with a friend.

When the Father does draw lines of dividing, he continues after a moment, *they are pure lines, without breadth, and thus invisible to human eyes. So you see, the Father's lines cannot be known by man, and they who make such an attempt their business are bound to err.*

———

We walk on with Jesus in silence a good while. Suddenly we realize that we have walked a great distance from the mansion. The terrain has changed. The greenery here is not nearly so lush. The high waters are already thinning, and less of their emerald color sparkles now in the grasses and leaves.

Nor are we walking alone. Many others are about. The way is actually growing crowded, with considerably more bustle and activity than higher up. We are greeted as we pass. Everyone knows Jesus and speaks familiarly with him, and once again we notice the containers they are carrying.

Suddenly with alarm we realize the air is changing too. The crisp atmosphere of the mansion region has begun to give way to the old familiar feel of the valley fog. We had forgotten its feel! Have we left the estate? we wonder. There has been no visible fence or gate!

Then we realize that we have been descending all morning as we walked!

Where are we going? we ask in some anxiety. You're not taking us back to the valley!

Have no fear, Jesus reassures us. *There were many questions on your mind earlier. We are going to visit some of the low-lying borderlands, where you will find answers to them.*

Did you not say that the borders of the estate were far away?

They are. These are not "borderlands" because they are near the boundaries, only because they are far down the slopes from my Father's home. They are the frontier out-posts of the estate, lying in the fringe regions. But we are still very much within the precincts of the estate.

Who are all these people?

Your brothers and sisters, my Father's own sons and daughters.

They are part of his family?

Yes, certainly.

Then why do they live so far out here, so far down in the lowlands?

They choose to.

But why? It's not nearly so pleasant, and the air is not at all invigorating.

That is a puzzle. But they appear to be more comfortable down here.

We cannot imagine it. Especially since they seem familiar with the mountain places.

Why do you say that? asks Jesus, responding to our thought.

Because they are walking up and down, and so many of them were back there earlier.

They sojourn there, it is true. But they do not have eyes to see the mansion for what it is. They merely conduct their business and then return. Their lungs are not accustomed to the high air.

By their business, do you mean those containers they all have?

Yes.

What are they?

They are gathering water from the wells and pools outside the mansion, where accumulates some of the over-

flow from our Father's springs, to take back down to where they live.

But we understood there was room enough for all the Father's family up there . . . in the mansion itself.

Oh, there is. Vastly more than sufficient room for all who would dwell there.

Why don't they then?

They would rather cart the meager containers of water down the hill, and come back for more when they need it, than to go inside and live where they can drink of it constantly. As I said, it is a puzzle, and it grieves our Father. But such is their choice, and until they decide otherwise, there is little anyone can do to dissuade them.

But can't they be told? Surely if they only knew what it was like inside the great room they would—

They have been told. In a thousand ways. All have been told. You should understand. You were once of their number. You lived many years in the valley. Telling is not required . . . only hearing.

But this is not the valley. We thought we were still within the Father's estate.

We are. But the valley winds in and among the hills and mountains to great lengths, like the inlets of the sea. You will find many, many pockets of valley dwellers in our Father's family too. Of the places I will show you, some lie higher on the slopes than others. But some, sad to say, are so low as to be quite as suffocated by valley fogs as the main part of the valley itself. Those who make their home in such parched regions find the high air so difficult to breathe that they must make quick work of it when they venture up to gather the water they need, almost holding their breath until they get back down.

That is beyond belief. The air up there is so much easier to breathe!

Not for them. They have so accustomed themselves to various fictional fabrications of their theologies, calling our Father by so many names of their own devising, that when they get too close to the reality of his presence of love, they find it difficult to breathe.

But why—we cannot understand it!

Because they cannot breathe the valley fog and the high air of our Father's love both at the same time. One must be left so that the other may be drawn in to full capacity. A few, like you, taste the high air and instantly the thought of the fog filling your lungs becomes loathsome. But many others find it just the opposite. They cannot stand the sting of accountability that the high air causes, and they hold their breath until they can retreat to the lowlands. Their comfort is found in the traditions of their valley elders.

We walk on, thinking about all he has said.

Looking up after some time, we find ourselves

approaching what appears to be a rather heavily inhabited settlement. As we walk into it, everyone greets Jesus with relieved and appreciative smiles of thankfulness.

They seem on the most intimate of terms with him, though we cannot help but notice the anxious looks they continually cast up the mountain in the direction from which we have come.

30

LOW-LYING
BORDERLANDS

The eternal home where the heart of the
Father makes his abode, and which he invites
all to share with him, exists only in the
innermost chamber of the mansion—
that room where love, goodness, and
trustworthiness dwell.

The Father sends us out with his Son,
throughout the entire grounds of his vast estate,
making sure we are familiar with all the other
parts of his nature; yet when that instructional
part of his business is done, he always brings us
home to his heart, to the truest and deepest and
highest attributes of his character.

The Father's kingdom includes many

low-lying border regions where his people
choose to make their homes. All do not live in
the high country.

Though all are invited to live in that home
of love, goodness, and trustworthiness, many
feel more comfortable in the cities of fear,
justice, grace, forgiveness, atonement, or in
the villages of justification, predestination,
omnipotence, sanctification, omnipresence,
wrath, or end times. And some attempt to
scale the impossibly high slopes of Mount
Holiness before the time is appointed for
them to do so.

———————

We have seen that *fear*, properly understood according
to the Father-child relationship of Genesis 2, is the
beginning of a proper relationship of nonindependent
childness toward our Father.

But are we to *live* in that part of his kingdom where
fear is the prevailing perspective?

As a place from which to start our upward journey, fear points an accurate direction. As the abode

for a complete spiritual perspective—a thousand times no!

Fear is a mere beginning point!

What about the village of *omnipotence?* Is it a place flowing with milk and honey?

God *is* omnipotent without question. But scratching out an existence while attempting to live only in that desolate corner of his kingdom is difficult indeed.

Oh, friends, why do our dear brothers and sisters want to live where provision is so scant! So little food is to be found in the environs of the village of omnipotence, and a kind of living starvation often results for those intent to remain there. No one in that place has the faintest idea what the word *Abba* means.

Nearby sits another village called *omnipresence.* Is it a portion of the kingdom where comfortable dwellings can be built?

More to sustain life tends to grow there, and on the whole its residents are much healthier than the citizens of omnipotence. Yet the place still makes for an incomplete and superficial sort of life.

Is *justice* part of God's being? Of course, the Bible tells us so.

But he does not want us establishing our home *in* his justice, though many Christians do.

Oh, but I feel bad for the residents of justice. It must be such a somber and chilly place!

The ground there is hard, and the only food it is able to produce contains a certain sourness that takes away a good deal of the pleasure of eating.

The elevation is low, too, affecting the quality of air and making the region far more susceptible to the infiltration of valley fogs than is altogether healthy.

It lies far down the slopes, well away from the heart of the estate. Jesus visits from time to time, and the residents are always glad to see him, reminding themselves that he was "the necessary satisfaction for God's justice."

As far away from the living center as it is, however, many of the Father's sons and daughters choose to construct their homes in the city of justice, for land is inexpensive and building materials, though not of the highest quality, are readily available even to the most unskilled of carpenters. It is one of the ancient cities of the kingdom as well, with a long history that its residents feel qualifies it as perhaps the most important city of the land.

Is *wrath* an aspect of God's nature? Of course, the Bible tells us so.

But he does not want us making our home in the village of his wrath, though sadly many try to erect a chilly domicile there too.

Wrath is found upon the grounds of the Father's estate, and we do well to know its location and the causes for its incitement. But it lies at the bottommost point of all, on the very valley floor, though still part of the King's property. It is continually covered by the valley fog, and in that place the high mountains of Fatherhood are nearly entirely cut off from view.

Those in residence in that bleak, gray region still suffer from the illusion that the Master of the estate is an Ogre whom they must not get too close to. Oh, if only they could intimately know him!

When Jesus visits them, they sigh with relief, discussing ever and again their gratefulness for his "taking God's wrath on himself" but never seeing the tears in Jesus' eye that they so misunderstand his relationship with the Father.

It must pull at the Father's heart to see them

working so much harder than necessary to eke out an existence in those frigid and airless foggy wastes, barely surviving, when he has so much warmth to give them up at the mansion where his own heart dwells with his sons and daughters who have discovered the mysteries of its innermost chambers.

———

Is God's being full of *grace?* Of course, the Bible tells us so.

But he does not want us making our home *in* his grace either.

Grace lies on the other side of the estate, several days' journey from wrath and justice. In fact, grace is such a warm and cheerful and altogether cheery place that a great multitude have built homes there and are quite comfortable. It is one of the largest cities on the estate, with a more temperate year-round climate even than the mountaintop regions.

The ground there is softer and grows quite a number of things of itself, without requiring of much tilling. The city of grace sits higher on the slopes than many of the lesser villages, and more of the waters from above trickle down, though the green of them is paler than emerald.

But so little of the hard and vigorous work of the estate gets accomplished there. Seventh-day leisure is the predominant element of its spiritual creed. In truth, the city is in large measure a retirement community for many citizens of the kingdom.

There are expeditions to be mounted, both higher up into the distant hills still out of sight and back into the valley. There are fences to be attended to, battles with the great enemy to be waged . . . oh, so much to be done! The Father needs stouthearted and manly sons and daughters to be about his tasks.

Alas, not many such laborers and warriors come from the land of grace, for the food and air there do not produce stalwart and vigorous constitutions.

Those dwelling in grace are neighbors to those who have made *forgiveness* their chief place of residence.

The Son visits these cities more often than he visits the dwellers in wrath, but he still would rather they accompany him back to the home of his Father.

Those dwelling in forgiveness have great difficulty acquiring the strengthening exercise they need if they are to scale the summits of the estate.

Is *holiness* part of God's being? Most assuredly!

But he does not even want us making our home *in* his holiness.

Holiness is found on slopes of exceeding height on the distant borders of the estate. There is no village, no community of holiness, only a snowcapped peak by that name, so high it is invisible through the clouds that constantly surround it.

Many of the Father's own do live there, but they cannot scale that peak until the time for such ascension is ordained by the Father and he takes them there himself. There is no oxygen there for us. It is impossible for our kind to exist there. We cannot breathe the rarified air, for it requires new lungs to take it in.

Occasionally a visionary mortal tries to scale the sheer face of righteousness leading to Mount Holiness, but always with the same result. In truth, man cannot live there during his days of mortality. Those who insist upon trying are either injured in the attempt and eventually return to live out the remainder of their days in the valley, or else they tumble down time and again, back to the regions of grace and forgiveness.

There, after refreshment and fellowship with others of like mind, they once again summon the determination to have another go at the sheer cliffs where they are sure the heart of God dwells. Over and over they find themselves disappointed.

Certainly the Father will take us to gaze up the mountains of righteousness and holiness from time to time. As long as we keep hold of his hand, we will be able to breathe, however high up he chooses to lead us. He wants us familiar with the landscape there, for he says that someday we shall receive the new lungs and then we shall be capable of dwelling there with him and his Son.

For now, however, he does not encourage our futile attempts to live there. Only occasional quiet and hallowed excursions are allowed.

When we live *in* the Father's *love, goodness,* and *trustworthiness,* then will he make use of all the other attributes of his infinitely complex nature—according to their perfect, not partial, purposes; then will he reveal his *whole* Self and thus transform us steadily by degrees into sons and daughters who bear the stamp and image of his own personality and character. And then will we dwell in the mountaintop mansion—the Father's own heart!—in the center of his kingdom, there to live with all three, Father, Son, and Spirit, forever.

31
THE ANSWER
IS TRUST

Climbing back toward the Abba-mansion of
our new home at day's end, weary from the
excursion to the many communities and villages
of the lowlands, we find, to our delight, vigor
reviving our limbs the higher we go.

Those watching from the spiritual abodes in
the low-lying, border, and far-from-the-mansion
cities—those shivering, comfortable but
unsmiling, in wrath and justice, those with wide
smiles but atrophied spiritual muscles living in
grace and forgiveness, and those nearly dead
from the attempts on Mount Holiness—they all
look upon us with odd expressions, wondering
why we cannot perceive the vital aspect of the

Father's character where they make their homes,
which, each group says, is too pivotal to venture
away from even for a moment.

It must grieve the Father's heart to see them
huddled and cramped there when he has so
much room for them inside his mansion higher
up!

Suddenly we realize that the weariness we felt
was not from the climb up, but from the
disheartening journey down.

And thus another truth of the Father's
country comes clear: that most of the valley's
principles operate in almost exact reverse up
here. The higher we walk, the more vigor we
feel!

The way is quieter now as we climb. The
crowds and bustle and spiritual activity grow
less.

The gentleman Jesus, kind and wise elder
Brother that he is, allows much room for
reflection. He knows the solidification of all the

discoveries we are making takes time. Neither his nor the Father's purposes can be rushed.

Jesus has shown us many things. Much occupies our mind and heart. Whole new foundations must be laid upon which to base what we have previously called our "faith."

"What about punishment of sin?" we suddenly find ourselves asking after a long silence.

The question startles even us. We hadn't realized it was lurking so near the surface.

"If love is the highest, then . . . ?" But our words trail off and the question remains unfinished.

Jesus smiles.

I am not surprised to hear you ask it, he replies.

"Why . . . I don't understand."

Perhaps the most common reproach leveled by the lowlanders against those who have made their home in my Father's heart is that they are putting aside his hatred of sin in order to take up residence in his love. It is a great fallacy of thinking among the fogbound who have not fully beheld the three peaks of my Father's being, but examine only the outer husks surrounding their truth.

To answer you: Our Father MUST eradicate sin from the world. His holiness can never tolerate its evil. This necessity is why he sent me among you, why I went to the cross. He hates sin. If punishment is required to annihilate it from the universe, verily will he send his righteous punishment.

"From all the places we visited, and from what you said about his wrath and justice being smaller than his love, and how they were all taken up in the greater characteristics of his nature, does that mean that the punishment of sin is perhaps less severe?"

Where did you hear a falsehood like that? The words fall quickly from Jesus' lips.

"I thought perhaps—"

You thought his love, because it is the loftiest peak of all, infinitely higher than our Father's justice, would therefore erase the requirement that sin be atoned for?

"There were those in the lowlands, when they found I had made my home in love, and love only, who implied that I believed such things."

They often think it of those who dwell in the divine home amongst the peaks. One of the trials that must be borne by the heart-dwelling children is that their own family so little understands their special fellowship with the Father. Opposition to the discoveries made in the inner rooms of our Father's mansion is to be expected.

"Opposition by our own brothers and sisters?"

Them most of all.

"But why? I cannot see why it should be so."

A smiling Father threatens their established theologies. They take a valley gratification in representing every characteristic of my Father's nature as rooted in what they call his holy hatred of sin. His normal posture, to their distorted view, is angry and stern. Their small god is so preoccupied with his own holiness that his children can find no room in his heart wherein they may dwell, no smiles within his gruff personality with which to light the dark paths of their gray world. Remember, the city of justice is one of the most ancient of the borderlands, with more deeply entrenched traditions and theologies than any of the others.

These things sadden me, for those of such outlook pay so little heed to what I have told them of the larger and more encompassing nature of their Father. But my Father loves them dearly, even in their shortsightedness, and is constantly doing all he can to turn their eyes toward his heart of love.

Be not anxious about what they say. Their eyes are simply unable yet to penetrate above the fogs. Give me time with them. I visit them often and am busily engaged in trying to point their gaze upward.

"But what of the things they say? I want to know all truth, not only the loving side."

That is why we will continue to make excursions throughout the Father's estate, so that you will grasp the fullness of his nature and not just portions of it. But you can only understand the wider extent of our Father's nature and purposes if your home is in the chamber of love.

"Is there truth, then, in their theologies?"

Of course. Truth exists in all the places we have visited. Incomplete truth, it may be, but truth indeed. You have seen the fire in his eye, have you not?

"Yes, the warmth of love. I saw it immediately when you took me to him."

To you, who approached him with humility and submission and the heart of a child, the fire that shone from his eyes was love. You have spoken truly. But to those who rebel against him, who listen to the serpent and his demons, who set their face contrary to the Father's purposes, that fire is a consuming fire indeed. I have not shown you all there is to see, and there is just such a place as the old legends speak of—a place where the fire rages and the worm dieth not.

"On the estate?" we ask in alarm.

Far over the peaks, many ranges of mountains distant.

"Who lives there?"

Those from the valley who refuse every invitation to come to my Father's kingdom in the mountains.

"Will you show us those places too?"

Ah, little one, not everything is for you to see at present. If I took you there, you could not understand how the fire of love you beheld in our Father's eyes is the same inferno that rages in that lowland. All things cannot be opened to you while you are yet a mortal.

"A place such as you speak of seems so different from the wonderful room where the emerald waters flow."

As different as black is from white, as different as rebellion is from obedience, as different as death is from life. You have indeed perceived it correctly. The look of love in his eyes is always the same, but by necessity it must express itself through different manifestations.

"It is so hard to understand."

When the Father speaks sternly, heed his commands. For truly will those who persist in willful and intentional sin discover his anger. The Father is full of love. Love is his very essence. But the fire that burns in his eyes contains no flames of mere earthly consequence. For the closer those who, by choice, have made themselves his children draw into those flaming eyes, the more they are consumed by his love. Those who resist their own childness, however, feel the burning of what must seem to them the very opposite of love.

He is no tame God. Our Father's commands must never be toyed with. The consequences of permanent rebellion against him are eternally life threatening. Hell is no fantasy, but the burning repository of all sin. Do not forget, young one, I have been there. Make no mistake, punishment of sin and the hell necessary to carry out that end, is as intrinsic to our Father's design as are the waters of life that flow from the inner chambers of his mountain home.

"But I still don't understand. If love swallows all, how then—"

Ah, young one. Put away the algebraic formulas of the valley. The equal signs fall differently up here. All the equations are redrawn when you leave the valley. There is no either-or with our Father. All must be accomplished . . . all must be fulfilled. Sin must be atoned for. My sacrifice must be brought to completion. Love swallows all, but erases nothing.

"But I don't see how—"

Of course you don't. Your eyes are only beginning to see.

Words fail us, and we realize instantly the incorrect direction of our thoughts in attempting to equate the seeming disparities of the Father's nature according to valley appearances of likeness.

My young brother, place no limits of creaturehood upon the Father's love in any of the multifold directions in which it expresses itself. None of his attributes, none of his divine purposes will disappear from the face of creation without being fulfilled. None. The infinitude of our Father's love is no human love. No man or woman loves sufficiently to discern how righteous justice is to be brought to the aid of fulfilling that love. But our Father is subject to no such mortal limitations. His love will accomplish all.

Jesus sees how full our heart is, trying to take in the enormity of all he said.

Fret not over the dilemma these things pose to your human mind, my young brother, he says. *All is well.*

You may trust our Father! He is absolutely and utterly trustworthy in all things, in all ways, and for all the men and women of his creation!

We can say no more, for we are pondering, as did his own mother, all these magnificent truths in our heart.

32

A HIGH VIEW . . .
AND MORE LOFTY
VISTAS AHEAD

Do you think perhaps our journey to the
mountain regions—following in the footsteps of
that ancient stranger who visited the valley with
tales of high places—has not really advanced us
many miles?

But it has. We have climbed steadily upward,
over some rugged and previously unexplored
territory.

And now, as we pause to look back down
over the valley and low borderlands from which
we came, we indeed discover that our whole
vantage point has shifted.

The circle walkers of the valley and foothills
come into our sight now and then in their

bustling travels, and they do seem to be covering much more ground than we have. Ah, but would we trade places with them?

Would we trade their distances logged, or the checkoffs marked in the boxes of their informational charts, for the wondrous high views we have had?

What makes the outlook from the high places of Fatherhood so spectacular is not so much how far we have come, but the still higher and more breathtaking views we have begun to catch sight of up ahead.

"But our journey together is nearly done," you say. "I am eager to continue, but it is clear you are almost through."

It is true, the time has come for us to part company.

It is necessary that we do so. The Fatherhood of God remains inexhaustible, and the discoveries awaiting you as you move toward those higher and deeper regions of intimacy with

him are discoveries into which he himself must
lead you.

As for me, I must now continue on my way
with our mutual Father, as he leads me, and
allows you to do the same. He will be a far more
faithful, more knowledgeable, wiser, and more
loving guide than I!

————

Yes, the time has come, dear friend and faithful companion, for us to pause a moment and reflect . . . to
look back over our time together.

Does it seem brief? Perhaps too brief?

In truth, my friend, we have traveled a much
greater distance in our quest than you may realize.

A huge treatise may seem at first to cover more
ground. But if the movement is over flat terrain, where
the footprints go round and round in so many circles
you have already traversed before, how far have you
really progressed in the end? It is possible to walk
twenty miles and get no farther than a block from your
own house.

Direction is more pertinent to progress than the

size of the chunks of ground passing beneath your feet. It is important to know where you are bound.

As you go, remember the principles we have discovered along the paths we have trod that have allowed us up into these regions where the Father's love dwells.

Continue to look up. Heed your instinct. It is the whisper of Fatherhood calling, reminding, urging, exhorting, inviting you into the intimacy of his presence.

Look for the Father in the quiet, hidden places. The divine fingerprint exists in all he has touched. His emerald waters imbue the whole universe with life. Do not look for *information;* instead, pursue the Father's *character.* He delights to reveal himself, but such revelation comes only to those who seek him. Open your eyes to *see.*

Putting fear in its proper perspective, neither reverencing it nor ignoring it, *follow God's Fatherhood to finality* in the three most fundamental characteristics of his being: His works are completely and only *GOOD,* you may *TRUST* him utterly, for what he is, is *LOVE.*

Make your home in the center of his mansion . . . *in his very heart.* Fill every corner, every cistern within you from the life-giving waters of his Fatherhood.

Travel with your elder Brother Jesus throughout his entire estate, learning about all aspects of the Father's being. But do not take up residence in any of the low-lying borderlands. *Live in the inner chamber of his mansion among the mountaintops, in his love, his goodness, and his trustworthiness,* and them only.

In all things, at all times, in every circumstance . . . *call him Father!*

Abba is the heart's cry of intimacy.

Truly, he is a God to call Father.

> *Our Father, we cannot adequately express to you our deep gratitude for what you have revealed to us about yourself. O God, reveal yet more! Open us to the fullness with which you desire that we see you. How can we ever thank you for being so good, so loving, so trustworthy toward us . . . toward all the sons and daughters of your creation? In truth, there is only one way: by entering more fully into the Fatherhood, which has been our destiny from the beginning.*
>
> *Fill the reservoirs within us with the waters of your being! Keep those waters fresh and life-giving by the continually renewed immediacy of your presence.*
>
> *Help us, Father. We are yet so small in our thinking, so blind to the magnitude of your love, so tenta-*

tive in our trust, so fearful of what your goodness might mean. We need your help so desperately!

Oh, but it is the deepest desire of our heart to walk in increased intimacy with you! Help us, we pray. Draw us, nurture us, guide our steps, keep hold of our hands, and lead us farther into that unbounded chamber of intimacy we desire but are too small to apprehend. We can take no step without you, so thorough is our dependence upon you.

Let us seek and rejoice in that childness, leaving behind the independence of the world's adulthood and entering into the divine childlikeness that allowed Jesus to be the Savior of the world. In truth, whatever is required, transform us into sons and daughters who reflect the image of your Son.

Reveal yourself to us, we ask yet again. Open our eyes to see you where your holy being shouts with divine silence. Guide our steps now as we continue on into the innermost regions of that chamber of your heart, which knows no end.

Thank you, Father, that we can make your heart our home.

Thank you, above all, that we have learned to call you Father.

Additional titles from Michael Phillips

THE SECRET OF THE ROSE
Don't miss this masterfully written drama of a noble Prussian
family's plight during World War II and its aftermath!

#1 The Eleventh Hour   0-8423-3933-7
As Baron von Dortmann's faith is ultimately tested by
Nazism, his young daughter, Sabina, befriends the American
Matthew McCallum—a relationship soon to be torn by war.

#2 A Rose Remembered   0-8423-5929-X
In the midst of Cold-War Berlin, Sabina relentlessly
searches for her imprisoned father—while hiding from a
man she almost married.

#3 Escape to Freedom (New! Fall 1994)   0-8423-5942-7
Desperately eluding their pursuers, Sabina and Matthew
seek a way to get her father out of Communist Germany.
Will they find the freedom to love as well?